D1603567

Prudent Advice
for Every Woman

Prudent Advice
for Every Woman

Jaime Morrison Curtis

Andrews McMeel
Publishing

Kansas City · Sydney · London

For Scarlet, Joleen, Niko, Clare,
Quinn, and Madison

A ship in harbor is safe,
but that is not what ships are built for.

— John A. Shedd

Introduction

Like many mothers, after my daughter was born I found myself in the hormonal haze of new love and sleepless disassociation. Bleary, bloated, and preoccupied with a notion of impending loss, my particular anxieties formed themselves into a sort of tunnel—an inescapable shot from point A (my sudden and overwhelming sense of responsibility) to point B (my certainty that I could not fulfill that responsibility). As my attachment to my baby grew deeper, the channel only grew darker, narrowing until it began to consume me with a pointed suspicion that something was about to go horribly wrong. An irrational, but very real, distress grew inside of me. It manifested itself as an almost obsessive fear that I would pass away, leaving my young child motherless, unintentionally, yet unavoidably, abdicating the one true responsibility I had ever known—my duty to raise her. And so I woke every day (every two hours, in fact) with a sinking feeling that our dewy bubble of love would burst and my worst fears would be realized—the most final evidence that I could not fulfill my duties would come to pass. Aware that this sensation was on its way to robbing both myself and my young daughter of the joy of our new family, I set out to conquer it. My first step was simply to write. As the words fizzled across the page like so many champagne bubbles, feelings of promise, hope, and, surprisingly, congratulations started to surface. I allowed myself a small amount of praise for having birthed her, and saw her in a new light: as a woman-to-be who had made her way into the world. Somewhere between my first written words and the final 500 pieces of prudent advice, my anxiety evaporated, and in its place a sense of purpose emerged.

I felt a compulsion to record for her my deep love, as well as the hopes and expectations

I had for her. I wanted to gather lessons from her aunts, grandmothers, and great-grandmothers that would encapsulate for her the tools that could assist her in finding her own happiness. Whether regarding politics, friendship, or simply doing laundry, I wanted to share with her the collected knowledge of her family's women and dive into my own head to put into words the things I had learned and hoped would benefit her. Through this process, I ascertained that so many of life's lessons for young women boil down to the core values of thoughtfulness and generosity, but they often seemed quaint or even irrelevant in today's context. For my unique daughter, I needed to create a fresh take on how to apply those universally respected qualities to the large and small challenges of life as a woman today.

So I created a list of prudent advice for my baby daughter. Many women saw my list as a seed, an invitation to contemplate their own legacy to their families and to share it in the present. I believe that is a worthy effort that will reward any woman. By having access to this assembled wisdom, girls will know the depth of consideration and love they were given, and as a result will have a solid springboard into their own independent lives, as well as a soft place to land at home.

It is possible, if not likely, that I may still fail my daughter, but I have found some peace knowing that I tried, with every particle of intention I could summon, to show her she was considered, loved, and imbued with a sense of responsibility to herself and to this world. My hope is that as you read this book, alone or with a young woman you love, the wisdom collected within will bring you similar repose.

1

Always send a thank-you note.

This has served your mother and grandmothers
well for generations and seems a fitting
place to start.

2

**Try to know what is bubbling around
inside your heart.**

Your heart is a great river after a long spell of rain,
spilling over its banks. All signposts that once stood on
the ground are gone, inundated and carried away by
that rush of water. And still the rain beats down on the
surface of the river. Every time you see a flood like that
on the news you tell yourself: That's it. That's my heart.

—*Kafka on the Shore*, HARUKI MURAKAMI

3

**Don't underestimate your father's
ability to understand you.**

Or any man's for that matter.
Set high expectations.

4

**When given the opportunity,
wear a costume.**

5

**Learn to love cooking if you can.
If you can't, still have a few simple dishes
that you can prepare well.**

Asparagus Wrapped in Bacon

Cut the hard bottoms off the stalks of a bunch
of asparagus.

Wrap four pieces of asparagus in one piece of bacon
and secure with a toothpick that has been soaked
in water. Repeat with remaining asparagus.

Sprinkle generously with coarse salt.

Grill over medium heat until the bacon is crispy
and the asparagus is browned.

6

Wash your face twice a day.

And apply moisturizer with sunscreen.
Nice skin will be important to you someday.

7

**Make time for the art museum
in every city you visit.**

You learn much about a city and yourself
when you see its art collection.
A good museum will fill your chest until it feels
as though your heart could explode.

8

**A dog is a loyal friend from whom you will
learn the nature of love and devotion.**

9

Give lots of hugs to everyone you care for.

This is one of your father's most
endearing qualities.

10
Offer your seat to elderly and pregnant people.
And help them with their bags.

11
Thank those who offer you assistance in their native language.
Thank you, *Danke, Merci, Gracias, Grazie, Gratia, Efcharisto, Obrigada, Xie Xie, Arigato, Mamnoon, Tak, Köszi, Khawp khun, Dakujem, Toda, Köszönöm, Mahalo, Mese*

12
Whenever possible, take the train.

13
You have a garden.
If you ever get sad that you don't have a garden of your own, remember that you have hundreds of beautiful gardens all over the city and all over the world. Try to erase the language of "want" from your head. You have everything that you need.

14
Appreciate the weather.
It is one of the few uncontrolled experiences of nature you will have if you live in the city.

15
Tip the person who handles your luggage.

16
Call if you are going to be late.
But try to be on time.

17
Be generous.
With your time, your money, your heart. If, on my best day, there was a single lesson I could hope to impart to you, this would be it.

18
When you are a preteen, read *Little Women*, *Little House on the Prairie*, and *Gone with the Wind*.
I have been saving my copies for you since I was a young girl myself.

19

If you have a daughter who can't sleep, sing "In My Life" to her.

This is your favorite lullaby. You gently pat my face with your tiny hands while I sing it to you, and by the end of the second round you are asleep. John Lennon wrote this in 1964, the year after his son Julian was born. It is my personal opinion that he wrote it thinking of his baby, and when I hear it or sing it, I think of you.

20

Your beauty is not something you earned; appreciate it but maintain modesty and humility about it.

Few things are as unattractive as a pretty woman who flaunts her assets in a boastful manner. Few things are as sad as a pretty woman who believes her beauty defines her worth.

21
Pay attention to politics.
There is so much I have to tell you about this subject, but for now I will advise you to register to vote, and then to vote in every election to which you are entitled, no matter how small. Perhaps you will grow up with a deep conscience and strength of conviction that will drive you into political life yourself. I am more certain than ever that you could succeed on that path. Regardless, you are obligated to participate in your own governance.

22
Learn the rules of football.
I wish I understood it.

23
**When frustrating things happen,
keep them in perspective.**

It's easy to let frustration over small
inconveniences and minor affronts mutate into
anger toward others and a general dissatisfaction
with life. If you can learn to manage this natural
tendency, you will possess a broad sense of
well-being and superior mental and
physical health.

24
Don't lie, except to comfort people.

I'm not upset that you lied to me, I'm upset
that from now on I can't believe you.

—Friedrich Nietzsche

25
**When growing herbs for cooking, plant the
mint in a separate pot or it will take over
wildly and crowd the others out.**

26
Tend to your friendships, especially those with women.

Each friend represents a world in us, a world possibly not born until they arrive, and it is only by this meeting that a new world is born.

—Anaïs Nin

27
Take care of your teeth.

This is an incredibly boring piece of advice, but tooth pain is terrible, and unattractive teeth lead people to believe you are uneducated.
That's just how it is.

28
Splurge on fresh flowers once in a while.

Three hydrangeas in a low vase, some blue iris and big yellow sunflowers, or your grandmother's favorite, lilies. Any flower will do and will be a burst of color and a sweet-smelling start to your weekend. My favorite is ranunculus, with its sculptural stem.

29
Avoid smoking cigarettes.
It is extremely difficult to stop, and it will reduce your quality of life, especially when you are old.

30
When your clothes match your eyes you look especially pretty.

31
If you are out to dinner with friends and get stuck with a bill that is more than you owe, just pay it and don't give it a second thought.
You are lucky to have friends to eat with, and it's better to be the one paying than the one shorting the bill.

32
Forgive your mother.
I know I am likely to screw you up in some deep, painful way. But I am going to try hard not to.

33
Consider choosing footwear appropriate to the occasion.

For example, it is smart to wear boots in the rain and flip-flops in the sun, not the other way around. This is one of those "do as I say, not as I do" types of recommendations.

34
Good lighting is the key to decorating a cozy home.

35
Maintain your car according to the manufacturer's instructions.

Get oil changes on time, check the tire pressure—that sort of thing. When I was younger I couldn't be bothered with this stuff and learned my lesson the hard way, numerous times. It is unfortunate to feel like a cliché about women, and it is also unfortunate to have a malfunctioning car because of your own inattention.

36

It's easier if you clean as you go.

37

**Whole grains and fresh fruit
are good choices.**
But a cupcake is worth every calorie.

38

Sometimes people just want to be heard.
So it is important to learn how to listen.

39

**Well-manicured hands are not a necessity
but they can make you feel nice.**

40

**Try to use people's names when you
address them, even if you are fairly certain
you are never going to see them again.**
The gentleman who prepares your coffee and
the woman who hands you your valet ticket
are two examples. I have found that people feel
good when you acknowledge them in this way.

41
Maintain good credit at all costs.

This is a lesson for the ages. There is much more to it that I will do my best to teach you, but you can start by keeping a written budget and developing a sense of responsibility toward your future self.

42
Visit the important cities of the countries neighboring yours.

Such visits will help you gain insight into the experience of your neighbors who may be immigrants from that area. It will also be fun.

43
Don't be afraid to get lost.

When you're young it can be scary to find yourself in strange surroundings, but when you grow older and start to travel, you might find it liberating. It's a great feeling knowing that in the midst of a foreign landscape you are capable of finding your way back home, all by yourself.

44

Goals score points, but passing wins games.

When playing soccer, know where your
teammates are at all times, even before you
receive the ball, and understand that you don't
have to touch the ball to contribute to the goal.
This advice holds true for all team efforts.

45

Seasonal vegetables are tasty.

Butternut Squash with Lime

Preheat oven to 400 degrees Fahrenheit. Peel one
butternut squash and slice it into half-inch thick
pieces. Arrange the pieces on a baking sheet and
drizzle with the following:

2 tablespoons melted butter

2 tablespoons olive oil

Juice of one lime

Sprinkle with salt and pepper. Turn the pieces to coat.
Roast for 20 minutes. Turn them over and roast for
another 15 to 20 minutes. Sprinkle with chopped
rosemary. Eat!

46
Call people at home only after 9 a.m.

47
Define a space for your work.
Virginia Woolf said that every writer needs
a room of her own. In other words, if you have a
desire to write, make art, or create anything—a
quilt, a song—you need to make a space in
your home and your schedule for that
work to happen, and you need to be
protective of that space.

48
**When something tragic happens
to someone you care about, do not ignore
them just because you don't know
what to say.**
Just offer your support and listen.

49
Avoid clichés.
You are too smart; you don't need them.

50
It's okay if a storm makes you scared.
It helps to cuddle up to somebody or something.

51
If you flip off other drivers on the road, you will usually feel stupid afterward.

52
Please, please don't obsess about your appearance.
Obsessing is okay, but do it about something valuable.

53
Listen to music around your house.
Your dad appreciates music in such a powerful way that it is hard to understand what it does to him. You are part of him and, therefore, it is likely that listening to music will have the same effect on you.

54
Travel light.
When you are a little bigger but still a
young woman, all you will need to begin your
worldly adventures are some comfortable shoes,
a warm jacket, toothpaste, and some books.
And learning from my own experience,
I guess I would supply you with an emergency
credit card. Leave the blow dryer and checked
baggage for business trips and traveling
after you have a baby.

55
Marriage is a big decision—one that you should make for yourself.
You may want to marry a boy, or you may want
to marry a girl, or you may not want to get
married at all, or you may get married five times.
That should be entirely up to you. Hopefully
when you are considering marriage,
the idea that anyone does not have a right
to it will seem absurd.

56
Majority rules, sometimes.

In the interest of fairness, people tend to rule in favor of the majority opinion. While this often makes sense, it's important to consider that the majority may have an unfair power over the minority. Despite greater numbers, the majority can be ignorant, malicious, or just plain wrong.

At times you will find yourself in the majority, whether by the accident of your birth or your deeply held convictions. Don't let that position blind you to the needs of those on the other side. The time will come when you are in the minority, and you will understand the burn of oppression.

57
There are some topics of conversation that a lot of people like to talk about, but very few people want to hear about.

In general, I suggest saving these topics for your close friends: your physical aches and pains, the contents of your dreams, intimate details of your personal relationships, whining of any kind.

58

A gift is someone's way of showing they care for you.

At some point you may receive a gift that you don't like. This happens to everyone. Please accept it graciously and never say anything negative to the giver. You will only hurt them when they were trying to please you. True graciousness reflects genuine gratitude for the consideration that a gift implies.

59

Drink tea!

60

Get enough sleep.

And try to let your mom get some, too.

61

Goat cheese is a good alternative to cream.

Zucchini and Goat Cheese Pasta

- **1 pound summer squash and zucchini, diced**
- **1 tablespoon olive oil**
- **I clove garlic, chopped**
- **1 pound pasta**
- **7 ounces goat cheese**
- **2 tablespoons lemon zest**

Sauté 1 pound of diced summer squash and zucchini in a tablespoon of olive oil until the moisture has evaporated. Add a chopped clove of garlic in the last minute or two. Boil pasta, drain, and return it to the hot pot with a cup of the cooking water. Toss the pasta with 5 ounces of goat cheese. Serve the pasta with the sautéed squash, more crumbled goat cheese, and 2 tablespoons of lemon zest.

62

Take walks.

Walking is healthy for your body and your brain, especially when the weather is just right.

63
Don't build a case.

When a personal relationship is causing
you stress, be aware of your feelings and
communicate them instead of building a case
against the other person. For example, you don't
need to list the seven things the person did that
you didn't like, including the time he yelled at
the flight attendant, yawned while you were
speaking, or fell asleep while you were driving.
If you run off a list of errors you
believe someone has made, you will appear
judgmental and put him on the defensive.
You will also get into a detailed discussion of
each individual event rather than addressing
your feelings as a whole. It's more productive
to speak to your emotions through statements
like "I feel like you aren't enjoying my company,"
rather than the "case" you have built
against the object of your frustration. It's also
a way to keep yourself honest.

64
Don't hit people.
You will probably learn this when you are a little older, but for now, just take my word for it that it won't help you get your way.

65
When other people talk to you about their children, try to share their enthusiasm instead of just using the opportunity to brag about your own kids.
It is hard because your own children are the best in the world, but your dad and I have noticed most parents just squawk about their own kids and don't listen to one another! It is more fun to share the joy of parenting with friends when you are actually listening and genuinely care.

66
Throw parties!

67
Word is bond.

My choice of words will probably make
me sound so old to you, but my point is this:
Be a woman of your word. Your integrity is
the source of your self-esteem and the esteem
others hold you in. You may not always stick to
the most stringent set of ethical and
moral principles, but if you try to represent
yourself and your intentions truthfully, you will
sleep well most nights.

68
Wash your hair every other day.

Try not to wash it every day;
you can dry it out that way.

69
Know how to take a joke.

There are times when you just need to keep
it light and laugh at yourself, your situation,
or a simple, funny joke. On the flip side, don't
allow people to make racist, misogynistic, or
otherwise inappropriate jokes in your presence.

70

If you love a poem, passage, speech, or piece of prose, memorize it.

Then you will always have it with you.

71

Guilt is a paralytic emotion.

Guilt is not like shame, the experience of which teaches you something about your values. Guilt can be avoided in most cases by making a thoughtful choice and feeling confident in your decision. If you realize later that you've made the wrong one, absorb the lesson, make appropriate amends, then put it behind you. Being paralyzed by guilt serves no one well.

72
Keep a good karaoke song in your back pocket.

If you happen to have inherited your parents' inability to sing very well, that's okay—you should still sing all the time! Singing in the car or the shower or just humming to yourself while you walk is fun. Pick one song and learn to sing it really well. Then you can whip it out at karaoke night or some other occasion when singing seems like the thing to do.

73
Everyone kills his or her own lobster.

When cooking lobsters for friends, make it a rule that they can't eat a lobster unless they boil it themselves. That rule doesn't apply at restaurants.

74
A simple "No, thank you" is enough.

This is something I am not good at,
so I don't know quite how to put it into words
for you. I think many women, and especially
mothers, share this feeling of self-imposed
pressure to perform no matter what is asked
of them or to provide a rationale for declining.
You will inevitably learn that you can't give
everything to everybody all the time,
even if you want to. Whether it is your time,
your work, your money, your energy,
or your space, the only obligation you have
when someone makes a request is to consider
it thoughtfully and reply with honesty
and kindness. Sometimes that means saying
no, and if you can learn to say it without any
excuses, reasons, or apologies, you will be
a happy (and unique) woman.

75
Always RSVP.

I don't speak in absolutes too often, but this is
just decency. How wonderful to be invited!
Be courteous and respond.

76
Resist the urge to chop your hair off.

Short hair is completely adorable; my point is in
the "urge to chop" part. Usually, the impulse to
chop your hair off is about wanting a change in
your life that has nothing to do with hair. Then
you wake up the next day and everything is
exactly the same . . . except your hair.
That's when the tears start.

77
Sometimes it's just not about you.

Be aware of other people's important moments.
They aren't yours.
If you have the good fortune to be a part of the
big occasions of someone else's life, be sure to
let them shine and revel in their happiness!

78
Learn how to take a compliment.

Gracefully. Although being self-deprecating can be humorous, a genuine compliment deserves a genuine thank-you. Brushing off a positive observation isn't being humble; it speaks to an inner insecurity. Brush off enough compliments, and you'll find you stop getting them.

79
There is no substitute for baking soda.

Baking soda is a leavening agent that gives off carbon dioxide when it comes in contact with the acid in another ingredient. It fizzes and bubbles and creates the air pockets inside baked goods that make them light and fluffy. Baking powder contains baking soda and acid. If you use it instead of baking soda you need to use twice as much, and your end product will taste a little weird. Baking requires too much effort to settle for a funky end result, so if you're out of baking soda, don't try to substitute—head to the store or maybe ask a neighbor.

80

Not everyone is going to like you, and that's just fine.

81

Champagne is for sipping.

82

Anytime you are debating whether to shower or not, take the shower.

83

Sometimes you will feel alone.

It is a part of the human condition, and it is both inevitable and imperative that you experience this feeling. You will notice a variety of different responses to being alone: feelings like fear, relief, loneliness, desperation, even pleasure. All you can do is experience your solitude and observe your feelings about it.

In a Station of the Metro
The apparition of these faces in the crowd;
Petals on a wet, black bough.
                                —Ezra Pound

84

There is no such thing as "shallow."
People refer to others as "shallow" to describe
their values as superficial. "Superficial values"
is an oxymoron. You may have good reason to
believe that what is important to someone else
in fact isn't important at all, but slapping on a
label like "shallow" only highlights your own
inability to empathize.

85

**If you're asking yourself if you should have
one more drink, the answer is no.**

86
Some sentiments shouldn't be
taken literally.

These banalities are actually manifestations of
tender hopes that I have for you: "The world is
your oyster," "When you wish upon a star your
dreams come true," "If you believe in yourself
anything is possible." It is true you are tiny
and unblemished, and there is an avalanche of
possibility teetering under your munchkin feet.
But it's going to take more than wishing on a
star. I just want you to know that.

87
Wear a bra.

And make sure it fits properly. If it rides up
in the back, it's too big. If it cuts into your chest
in the front, it's too small.

88

Have fire handy.

There are many situations in which you'll be grateful to have matches or a lighter in your bag. Some examples: You get stranded somewhere and need to start a fire to keep yourself warm. You need to burn a thread to keep your seam from unraveling. You are in Italy, and the Italian police pull you over, and while the one policeman is checking your papers, the other one is trying unsuccessfully to light his cigarette.

89

When necessary, engage yourself in a rebellion against despair!

90

While washing nice dishes and glasses, put a towel in the sink.

That way if you drop one, it won't shatter. Your grandmother has nice china that may be yours one day, so take her advice.

91
Let it be.
Sometimes you just need to give it some time. It's hard to believe, but things really do tend to work themselves out, whether or not you are anxious about them.

92
Righty tighty, lefty loosey.
This handy mnemonic applies to any object that screws.

93
There's always room for one more at the table.
Just like there's boundless room inside your heart. Feeding people can be a reflection of how much you love them. At least for mothers.

94
**When attending a party, open the door
with one hand and bring a gift in the other.**

If it's a fancy party, make sure you have a good
story to tell when handing the gift over,
such as, "This wine is made by George
Clooney's brother," or "I picked this mint from
my garden, and it's great in mojitos."
If the party is being hosted in more humble
circumstances, you should bring something
practical, even toilet paper. (College party
hosted by your male friends? The girls in
attendance will appreciate it.)

95
Have a firm handshake.

This advice isn't just for boys. No reason to be
limp-wristed just because you're female.

96

If you don't have a lot of money for clothing, consider putting what you do have toward shoes.

Good shoes can make you look put together even with inexpensive clothes, whereas cheap shoes can drag down a good outfit. Also, shoes are one of the few things that usually increase in comfort as they increase in price.

97

Whimsy is essential.

You are a fanciful, playful girl. You bring back my sense of wonder about the world. Keep that with you as long as you can.

98

If you haven't worn it in a year, give it away.

Exceptions to this rule include jewelry and wedding dresses.

You are bound to experience disappointment.

Some people will tell you that if you never have any expectations, you will never be disappointed. Taken literally, that point is true. But the ability to remove all expectations from your psyche requires a Zen mastery that few people possess. I actually think it is important to have expectations. People, especially children, tend to rise to meet them. It's also about hope and hopefulness. Try to let disappointment be a learning experience from which you gather data about what is reasonable to expect, and don't let it mar your optimism.

The Darkling Thrush
I leant upon a coppice gate
      When Frost was spectre-gray,
And Winter's dregs made desolate
      The weakening eye of day.
The tangled bine-stems scored the sky
      Like strings of broken lyres,
And all mankind that haunted nigh
      Had sought their household fires.

The land's sharp features seemed to be
        The Century's corpse outleant,
His crypt the cloudy canopy,
        The wind his death-lament.
The ancient pulse of germ and birth
        Was shrunken hard and dry,
And every spirit upon earth
        Seemed fervourless as I.
At once a voice arose among
        The bleak twigs overhead
In a full-hearted evensong
        Of joy illimited;
An aged thrush, frail, gaunt, and small
        In blast-beruffled plume,
Had chosen thus to fling his soul
        Upon the growing gloom.
So little cause for carolings
        Of such ecstatic sound
Was written on terrestrial things
        Afar or nigh around,
That I could think there trembled through
        His happy good-night air
Some blessed Hope, whereof he knew
        And I was unaware.
                    —Thomas Hardy

100
I love you.
Your grandmother, my mother, asked that I share this with you here above all of her other gems. I can guarantee you, daughter, looking back on the relationship that she and I have shared, that there will be times you just don't believe it. But it is, and always will be, an absolute unwavering certainty that I love you.

101
Littering? No.
As you like to say: "Gross!"

102
Teach your baby the word "yes."
They learn "no" on their own so quickly.

103
If you apologize, know what you are apologizing for.
It's normal to screw up, and usually it's accidental. Just say you're sorry. But think about it for a minute first and make it genuine.

104

**The size of your breasts truly
does not matter.**

105

Politely but firmly question authority.
Except mine. Just kidding.

106

If you can, grow some of your own food.
Planting vegetables is good clear-your-head
time. Then nurturing and harvesting
them—with dirty hands and green all around
you—is rewarding in a way few things are.

107

**A handwritten letter exudes
warmth and class.**

108
Compliment people.

I don't mean you should flatter indiscriminately, but rather that you should express appreciation when it strikes you. Your father is a master of the genuine compliment because he is an observer. He will notice the unique thing about someone, and then he'll simply tell him or her how much he likes it. He'll compliment the security guard on how pretty her bracelet is, and I'll watch her face light up. With his example, I'm sure this will come naturally to you.

109
Nobody is looking at you like that.

If you're getting dressed and get caught in that "I have nothing to wear" circle of stress, it helps to remember that nobody is going to notice if you look a little off; they will all be too busy worrying about what they look like to care.

Keep your grandmother's cookie recipe alive.

Even if you don't love baking, make them
for me when I am old. Please.

Snickerdoodles

>   1½ cups sugar
>   ½ cup softened butter or margarine
>   ½ cup shortening
>   2 eggs
>   2¾ cups all-purpose flour
>   2 teaspoons cream of tartar
>   1 teaspoon baking soda
>   ¼ teaspoon salt
>   2 tablespoons sugar
>   2 teaspoons cinnamon

Preheat oven to 400 degrees Fahrenheit. Mix the
sugar, butter, and shortening. Beat in the eggs one at
a time. Stir in the flour, cream of tartar, baking soda,
and salt. Shape dough by teaspoonfuls into balls. Mix
the sugar and cinnamon together, then roll the balls in
it. Place ½ inch apart on an ungreased cookie sheet.
Bake 8 to 10 minutes, then immediately remove from
the cookie sheet. Makes about six dozen.

111

Root for other people.

We all tend to envy other people's successes.
It's not intentional; somewhere in our DNA it
seems to be programmed that for every success
for someone else, there is one less success for
us. For every book published, there is one less
book we will publish; for every baby had, there
is one less baby for us to have. Of course, that
is illogical. Fight off those thoughts; there is an
unlimited amount of potential for everyone in
this universe. Championing others is kind, and
even more, it's a display of optimism that will
seep into you and color your view of this life.

112

You only need to call once and leave one message.

113
It's the rider's fault, not the horse's.

Riding is an art form that needs to be practiced if you want to perfect it. I am not a rider, but as a child I enjoyed horses as most little girls do. If you want to ride horses, remember that they are gentle animals despite their size. Post lightly rather than pounding with your weight; use your core muscles to balance rather than the reins; give it praise. When you feel frustrated, remember it is your instruction the horse is waiting on, and summon your wits to guide the animal compassionately. From the women I know who are passionate about riding, I've learned that riding a horse is an intimate friendship as well as a sport.

114
Dress appropriately for work.
Whatever your job is, choose clothes that
are correct for that workplace; namely,
attire that is safe, clean, and (at most
workplaces) free of cleavage. You might
feel as if your clothes are an expression
of who you are, and you want to be that
person even at work. But I have found
that "who you are" is often someone
who wants a promotion and a raise,
and that doesn't happen if your clothing is
inappropriate. It isn't about being pretty,
or what brands you wear, or which skirt
best reflects your inner self. It's just about
taking the focus off your clothes and
putting it on your work. If you aren't sure,
look at the way your boss dresses and
take a similar approach.

115

**It's not a good idea to weld
while wearing tights because
the sparks will burn holes in your
stockings and legs.**

116

**At the close of each day, fill your head
with thoughts of how lucky you are.**

Count your blessings; give thanks.
No matter what kind of day you have had,
you are a fortunate girl in one way or another.
Your father and I talk to each other every
night before sleep about what a magical
joy you are and what a lovely life we
have together. It's important to bring these
thoughts to the front of your brain; it cements
the little things that make life happy into
one cohesive positive outlook.

117

Know that we are all
connected by biology.

You are a tiny scientist. Every day you spend
inordinate amounts of time applying
the scientific method to anything you see,
touch, feel, taste, or hear, trying to figure out
what it's for, how it works, and (I think maybe)
what it means. Your eldest uncle is a biologist,
and he wants you to understand some simple
truths that will assist you in your quest for
understanding: All life is made of cells whose
basic structure is protein; the instructions for
making these proteins are in your DNA;
and your cells can read the DNA of any other
living organism on Earth. As a result,
every living thing is equally significant. On
this planet everything is connected. These are
facts—what they mean to you is something you
will have to decide for yourself.

118

It's true that some things are worth fighting for.

But I can't tell you what they are, little girl. Only you know that.

119

If you can't avoid an argument, at least avoid doing it in a public place.

120

Keep good olive oil and real vanilla extract in your pantry.

These are two simple ingredients that make a big difference in the way your food tastes.

121

Read the fine print.

Your signature on a document still means something. It means you have obligations that can be enforced in court. The smaller the print and the more of it there is, the more likely something is being hidden. Read the document in its entirety, make sure you understand it, and negotiate changes before you sign anything.

122
Shakespeare is not boring.
You don't have to like it, but it's not boring.

We that are true lovers run into strange capers;
but as all is mortal in nature, so is all nature in
love mortal in folly.
—*As You Like It.* William Shakespeare

123
You don't have to pretend you know something if you don't.
It's okay just to say, "I don't know."
You can't know everything!

124
Go easy on the caffeine.
I am afraid I have not set a good example
in this regard.

125
You are an American.

Whether or not you agree with every
government policy, please don't take it for
granted that you are a citizen of the
United States. There is so much to be proud
of, including your right to be passionate
about your love of country, or to be vocal
about your disapproval.

126
Forks and napkins on the left, knives and spoons on the right.

It's not really a big deal, but that is how
a traditional place setting works.
Wine glasses also go on the right.

127
Clean up after your pets.

If you want the rewards that come with owning
a dog, you have to clean up your dog's poo.
Don't leave poo lying around where people
can step in it. That's disgusting.

128
Stand on the right; walk on the left.
In Europe, this is the rule (posted on signs) on elevators and sidewalks; people who are in a hurry move on the left, people who are not stand on the right. In the United States, it's a little less obvious, so I just wanted you to know that's how it works.

129
The trick to sewing in a straight line is a rubber band.
Wrap a rubber band around the base of your machine at the distance from the needle you want your hem to be. If you watch the needle while you sew, your stitches will look like you were sewing through an earthquake, so focus on the rubber band.

130
Order the local specialty.
Cheese curds in Wisconsin, arepas in Venezuela, banh bao and pho in Vietnam; the list is endless.

131

You are the wellspring of your own hope.

No one (besides your mother) will be more invested in your emotional well-being than they are in their own. Joy is not something gifted to you by other people; it's an outlook on the world that you have to cultivate independent of friends and lovers. Daughter, if I could give it to you, I would, a million times over, but the truth is that you are singularly responsible for your own happiness.

132

Magic is real.

133

There are times you need to listen to the same song over and over.

It just means the song is helping to access something inside of you that you couldn't get to any other way.

134
You should want to be with someone who wants to be with you.

You can't strong-arm someone into loving you.
Learn to respect yourself enough to move on.

135
When you drop off someone at home, wait until he or she gets inside before driving away.

Just to be sure that person has keys to make it in safely.

136
Try to bring things into your home that you either need or love, and let the rest go.

137

Understand that civil rights are the foundation upon which your life is constructed.

With this faith we will be able to work together, to pray together, to struggle together, to go to jail together, to stand up for freedom together, knowing that we will be free one day.

—Martin Luther King Jr., August 1963

138
Allow yourself to be moved.

To My Retired Friend Wei
It is almost as hard for friends to meet
As for the morning and evening stars.
Tonight then is a rare event,
Joining, in the candlelight,
Two men who were young not long ago
But now are turning grey at the temples.

. . . To find that half our friends are dead
Shocks us, burns our hearts with grief.
We little guessed it would be twenty years
Before I could visit you again.
When I went away, you were still unmarried;
But now these boys and girls in a row
Are very kind to their father's old friend.

They ask me where I have been on my journey;
And then, when we have talked awhile,
They bring and show me wines and dishes,
Spring chives cut in the night-rain
And brown rice cooked freshly a special way.

. . . My host proclaims it a festival,
He urges me to drink ten cups—
But what ten cups could make me as drunk
As I always am with your love in my heart?
. . . Tomorrow the mountains will separate us;
After tomorrow—who can say?

—Tu Fu

139
Shopping is neither a hobby nor a sport.

Shopping can be a fun activity; most women won't deny experiencing a little high when they find the perfect pair of three-inch aubergine leather heels to match that vintage paisley dress or a hand-stained mahogany hardwood end table that fits perfectly in the nook by the fireplace. But know that at the end of the day, shopping is simply a means of acquiring things. Life is not about amassing loads of material goods. When shopping becomes your hobby, it's time to find something else to fill the hole inside you where you normally put *stuff*.

140
Keep your wits about you.

When everyone else is freaking out, try to be the calm voice in the room.

141
See the beauty everywhere.

142
Get enough calcium.
Calcium is important for women, especially
when you are very young and very old.

143
Honor your grandparents.
They love you in a special way
that no one else can.

144
**The only problem you can solve
by eating is hunger.**

145
**The order that people should enter and
exit an elevator is this: the elderly, then
persons with disabilities, then children,
and finally able-bodied adults.**
Women before men in each category, and each
should hold the door open for the prior.

146
When someone asks how you are doing, reply and be sure to ask the same question in response.
Waiters and store clerks often ask "How are you today?" as a part of their jobs. Rarely does anyone think to ask them the same question in return. It helps to remember that they have lives beyond the immediate task of serving you.

147
Don't be afraid to use prodigious words.
Words are important and beautiful; so don't dumb down your thoughts because you think people will regard you as pretentious. There is nothing wrong with big words. Just make sure you know what they mean.

148
Fame is not something to aspire to.
Celebrity should be a by-product of talent, not a goal in and of itself.

149
People perceive things in 3-D.
There is no point in staring at yourself in the mirror examining what you look like from each angle. Your reflection is not multidimensional, but you are. Being comfortable with that is the most attractive thing in the world anyway.

150
Appreciate the crucial role that luck plays in the way your life unfolds.

I sometimes wonder: IF you and I had met under absolutely ordinary circumstances, and IF we had liked each other, what would have happened? If I had been normal, and you had been normal (which of course you are)?

—*Norwegian Wood*, Haruki Murakami

151
Let go.
Just let go on occasion.

152

Men, as a rule, are not good mind readers.

Articulate your thoughts to them clearly if you want to be sure that you will be understood. Imagine writing on a 3 x 5 card: short and to the point.

153

Spritz your succulents.

Succulents are wonderful plants if you don't have a green thumb (like your mama). They do well with little attention: Just wait until the soil is all dried out and then use a spray bottle to give them a nice shower instead of watering them.

154

You can talk to me about sex.

My parents didn't discuss sex with me very much, so I'm flying blind when it comes to communicating with you about this topic. I'm slightly uncomfortable and a little nervous that I'll say the wrong thing, but it's important to me that you and I can talk about this significant part of your life. I want you to know that you can ask me anything, and I will always tell you the truth.

You have responsibilities.

This is a big idea, little girl, but I know
you can handle it. I want you to realize that
as you grow you take on responsibility. In the
beginning, you are explicitly accountable for
items like your toys and your schoolwork.
As you age, your responsibility becomes more
implicit, expanding to include intangibles like
friendships and family bonds.
Whether or not you want this responsibility,
it exists; you have influence over everything
that you touch. Because I believe so strongly
that you are worthy of this responsibility,
I want you to embrace it. You have the capacity
to make moral decisions and are therefore
accountable to your choices. Those choices and
the example they set mean something to this
world, without ambiguity. You are of
great significance not only to me, but
also to yourself and to the world at large,
so act accordingly.

156

**Expressing your individuality
is important, but try not to become a
caricature of yourself.**

There is a certain knack to outwardly
expressing your personality. Things like tattoos
and purple hair can often reflect the opposite
of individuality, something more along the
lines of "I'm unique, just like all of my friends."
If you work too hard at using your outward
appearance to reflect your inner uniqueness,
you can seem one-dimensional.
Your individuality is illustrated by much
more than the way you look.

157

**If you want to leave a party and
you don't have a good excuse, spill
something on yourself.**

158

If you love someone, tell them.

And tell them often. It's a wonderful feeling to
be reminded that you are loved.

159
You reap what you sow.

I have always found this aphorism to be deeply touching. I don't believe it means you are responsible for all the good and evil you experience. Things will happen to you in this life that you do not deserve. I know there is random unkindness and pain that I won't be able to protect you from. But if you plant little seeds of goodness wherever you can, and you work to reflect light onto them, you will find that with the warmth of your effort and attention, they will reap abundant rewards. These rewards won't come wrapped in patterned paper, but they also won't disappear. If you neglect these opportunities, or if you use them to plant seeds of anger or disillusionment, you will regret it. Life can be unfair, but your deeds repay you in kind.

160

Indulge.

Live a rich life textured with little extravagances. Eat the hot fudge brownie, buy the handmade dhurrie rug, and lie in your flannel sheets all Sunday afternoon. Just remember that indulgence by definition is temporary gratification of a whim. Do it more than once in a while, and you're just a hedonist.

161

Live alone for a period of time.

I love living with you and your father; I also cherish the years I spent living alone. You shouldn't go from being someone's daughter to someone's wife to someone's mother without first being someone yourself. Living alone will allow you to discover who you are when no one is watching, what you need to get through a day, and, ultimately, that you are a capable, independent woman.

162
Mind your manners.

As a child, you may feel as though you're
required to submit to an arbitrary set of rules:
You are constantly told where to sit and what
to say and which fork to use. I want you to
understand the bigger reason for all this, even
beyond conforming to social norms. As an adult,
you won't be afforded the same latitude you
enjoy today to freely express your emotions.
When the tide of your own passion is so high
you're at a loss about how to behave, your
manners will guide you. They are the tool you
will use to maintain your dignity.

163
Learn how to drive a stick shift.

Don't worry, I'll teach you. I wish you could
have seen the look on your father's face when
we were in a tiny Venezuelan backwater and
the only way out was a stick-shift jeep that he
couldn't drive. Well, he can drive one now, and
I'll be sure that you can, too.

164
Overflow with passionate exuberance
every now and then.

Wild nights! Wild nights!
Were I with thee,
Wild nights should be
Our luxury!
Futile the winds
To a Heart in Port,—
Done with the compass,
Done with the chart!
Rowing in Eden!
Ah! the Sea!
Might I but moor
To-night in thee!

—Emily Dickinson

Beware your ego.

The egoism from which I should like to protect
you is not the constant tendency to be continually
and exclusively absorbed in our own interests
and to sacrifice to them the interests, rights, and
happiness of others. This egoism is incompatible
with any form of virtue, and even with any honest
feeling: it would be too much to bear if I felt it
necessary to protect you from such a feeling.

I am discussing the egoism which, in everyday
life, makes us see everything in terms of our
own health, our convenience, our tastes, and our
well-being; an egoism which keeps us in some
sense in the presence of ourselves, which feeds on
the small sacrifices it imposes on others without
feeling, and almost without knowing, their injustice;
an egoism, which finds whatever suits it natural
and just, and whatever harms it unjust and bizarre,
and which complains loudly about caprice and
tyranny if someone else, while humoring it, thinks
also of himself.

This failing diminishes benevolence and harms and cools friendship. We become dissatisfied with others, because their self-denial can never be sufficient. We become dissatisfied with ourselves, because our vague, aimless mood develops into a constant, painful feeling which we no longer have the strength to escape.

If you want to avoid this misfortune, ensure that the feelings of equality and justice become second nature to you. Expect and demand from others only a little less than you would do for them. If you make sacrifices for them, appreciate them for what they really cost you and not according to the fact that they are sacrifices. Seek compensation for them in your reason, which will assure you that they would be reciprocated, and in your heart, which will tell you that they do not need to be. You will find that life in society is more pleasant and, dare I say, more convenient, if you live for others. Only then do you truly live for yourself.

—*Advice to My Daughter*,
Marie-Jean-Antoine-Nicolas de
Caritat, Marquis de Condorcet

166
Watch *It's A Wonderful Life*.
I wanted your name to be Zsu Zsu. You can thank your father that it isn't.

167
There's no need to comment on anyone's weight.
Whether overweight or thin, it just makes people uncomfortable when you discuss their bodies. It's really none of your business anyway.

168
Take notice of pattern and symmetry.
These characteristics are universally appealing because they manifest an underlying order to our world. It's comforting.

169

Order whatever you want.

If you want a neon orange fruity cocktail with
a paper umbrella and plastic monkey hanging
from it, go for it! If you want a bowl of lettuce
with the dressing on the side, have one. Banana
sandwich? Be my guest. No one should judge
you by the style of food and beverage
you consume. If they do, eat with
someone else next time!

170

If you marry your first love
you will miss out on the exquisite
pain of a broken heart.

171

There is no "man's work."

You can change a tire, build a fire, take out the trash, invest your savings, fix the plumbing, and so forth. Now, if a nice man wants to help you with these things, and you want his help, by all means take it. You have nothing to prove; I just don't want you to count on a male human handling things for you that you are entirely capable of handling yourself.

172

There is "woman's work."

That work is having babies. No man can do it yet. And no man can ever truly understand what it is like to carry and birth a child. This is not something to blame them for, nor is it a point of pride: It's just a fact. Pregnancy and childbirth are singularly female experiences, just like fatherhood is singularly male. I'm telling you this only because in your life, even more so than in mine, you will believe that women and men should be fifty-fifty on everything, and if you choose to get pregnant you will realize that it just isn't so, and that it's also just fine.

173
When you're driving and someone lets you into their lane, thank them with a hand wave.

174
Extend your humanity to animals.
Any animal that you befriend or happen to encounter is deserving of your compassion and benevolence. What separates us from animals is only, arguably, sentience. Inasmuch as the laws of nature decree they are food, they are still entitled to lives of dignity.

175
If you are questioning whether someone loves you or not, the answer is right in front of you.

When it comes to [people] who are romantically interested in you, it's really simple. Just ignore everything they say and only pay attention to what they do.

—Randy Pausch

176
A wrap dress is universally flattering.

177
Introduce yourself to the neighbors as soon as you can after moving into a new place.

Getting to know your neighbors is a pleasure; if you're really lucky like your father and me, you may find some lifelong friends living right next door. Even if not, it still helps to have a cordial relationship; it allows you to beg their pardon if your dinner party is too loud or to ask for a spare egg if you need one.

178
The thing about makeup is you want to look like you aren't wearing any.

You really don't need to wear makeup, but if you want to (when you are older) that's fine. A coat of mascara and a little blush are the two cosmetics that work best to subtly accentuate your natural features. If you want to even out your skin tone with some foundation, just make sure it's the right shade and blend it well.

179
Talk to strangers.

Teaching you to fear strangers would be cynical.
The generosity of unknown people will ease
your burden on many occasions. Instead, I want
you to learn to gauge people's intentions by
listening to your gut instincts and recognizing
subtle cues. Confidence in this skill will allow
you to avoid the aberrant persons you encounter
and embrace something much more common—
the kindness of strangers.

180
Advocate for the causes you believe in.

Dante once said that the hottest places in hell are
reserved for those who in a period of moral crisis
maintain their neutrality.

—John F. Kennedy

181

Be where you are.

Try not to think about where you need to go next or where you just came from. This is more difficult than it sounds, but work at it. It's important for your head to be present in the place where your body is.

182

Unless you're playing a game, there's no point in keeping score.

Running a tally of who gets what in life will only frustrate you and annoy everyone else. It serves no purpose; the way life's benefits and hindrances are doled out will never make any sense.

183

Dance.

Rhythm, and by extension dance, are uniquely human characteristics—animals don't sway to music. Your body needs the physical and emotional release. It's essential that you not worry about what you look like while you're dancing; it would be a shame if you were so self-conscious that you couldn't let loose!

184

A calorie is a measurement of energy.

Just so you know the details: One calorie is the amount of heat energy required at a pressure of one atmosphere to raise the temperature of one gram of water one degree Celsius. What this means is that the more calories you eat, the more energy you have inside of you. When you don't use that energy, say by playing sports or cooking a meal on your feet, it is stored in your body as fat. A lot of people don't realize this; now you know that's how it works.

185

Get messy!

Some of the most joyous things in life
can be grimy, sloppy, dirty mayhem.
Gardening, baking, painting, camping,
childbirth: all glorious messes!

186

Relish rocking your baby to sleep.

Babyhood is so short and so infused with magic,
but it's also filled with exhaustion. There is
nothing on Earth as special as those restful
moments a parent shares with a sleeping baby
rocking in a chair, humming a lullaby, peacefully
nestled close. You are still a baby, and already
I mourn the day you grow too big to cuddle
on my lap as your tiny hands relax, your
eyes droop, and you drift off into safe,
contented slumber while I sigh at you,
delirious with love.

**A woman can run a country
(not just be a princess).**

See: Wu Zetian (China), Benazir Bhutto
(Pakistan), Mary McAleese (Ireland), Ellen
Johnson Sirleaf (Liberia), Angela Merkel
(Germany), Golda Meir (Israel), Aung San Suu
Kyi (Myanmar/Burma), Pratibha Patil (India),
Gloria Arroyo (Philippines), Tarja Halonen
(Finland), Michelle Bachelet (Chile), Helen
Clark (New Zealand), Margaret Thatcher
(Great Britain), Janet Jagan (Guyana).

188

Gambling is spending money to play games.

If you look at it this way, you'll be better able
to enjoy the entertainment of gambling on
special occasions. Just determine how much
money you are willing to spend to play craps
or blackjack with your friends for a few hours;
then when you've spent that amount you're
done. If you think of it as "winning" and "losing,"
gambling can easily become stressful, and some

people can lose control chasing good money after bad. They say the house always wins for a reason, so do yourself a favor and assume it won't be you who hits the jackpot.

189
Make tomatoes a staple of your diet.

They are both delicious and full of lycopene, which protects against heart disease and cancer. Serve them roasted as an appetizer for a dinner party, and your guests will swoon, despite how simple they are to prepare.

Roasted Tomatoes

Preheat the oven to 400 degrees Fahrenheit.

Cut several Roma tomatoes in half lengthwise and place them in a shallow baking dish. Douse them with a few tablespoons' worth of olive oil. Sprinkle with salt, pepper, and dried thyme. Crush a few cloves of garlic over the tomatoes. Roast for about an hour, until they are soft, and the skins are slightly charred. They will be fragrant and juicy. Arrange them on a platter and serve with sliced French bread and herbed goat cheese. Pesto also makes a nice accompaniment.

190
Your period isn't gross.
Menstruation isn't something to be embarrassed about; it's just a personal experience that we discuss discreetly. You'll get more comfortable with it as you get older.

191
Wear your seatbelt.
It's one of those things you aren't overly concerned with until you get older and your own mortality starts to gnaw at you. For now, do it because your mortality gnaws at me.

192

**Ensure that the "bad" things you do are
the result of your own choices.**

You are undoubtedly going to engage in some
unhealthy, unwise, or otherwise questionable
behavior somewhere along the line; this is part
of learning your limits and establishing your
comfort zone. Please have enough
self-awareness to at least make the conscious
choice to participate, rather than floating
through life getting swept up in whatever
trouble comes your way.

193

Leggings are not pants.

194
You won't inevitably end up just like your mother.

I don't know why people say this; it just isn't true. You are your own woman, and if you become a mother, you will clearly make your own choices. I'll tell you what my mother told me: When you start your family, simply pick the things I did that you liked and keep them and take all the things you hated and never use them.

195
Buy the Indian sari.

Hang it in the closet next to your Vietnamese ao dai, your Alaskan kuspuk, and your Guatemalan huipil.

196
Some things are best saved for another conversation.

Stay on point, don't try to cram too much in, and realize when the conversation is over.

197
Treat a cut of meat with tenderness and admiration.

Learn how to carve a chicken, bone a fish, and properly prepare the various cuts of beef. Show respect for the life that gives you sustenance.

198
Health care is not a right.

The way our constitution is structured you have an inalienable right to an attorney, a gun, a god, and due process. You do not have a right to be healthy, to a doctor, to medicine, or to equal access to care that could save your life or the lives of your children. Let this weigh heavily on you as you choose a profession and where to expand your political leanings and charitable giving.

199

Wear bikinis while you can!

There will come a day when you realize that you've traded in your youthful body for a whole other one; you'll look down at yourself and think "When did this happen?" That's the day a bikini stops being appropriate. Don't worry about that day—I promise by the time you get there, you really won't mind—and in the meantime have a blast in adorable two-pieces.

200

Take only what you need.

When things are free, it's easy to overindulge. If you take ten bananas because the bananas are free, you'll likely end up with eight rotten bananas covered in flies while another person is left tragically bananaless. Take what you're going to use and leave the rest for someone else.

201
There's no need to give disclaimers.

When you present your work (a research paper, a painting, a song), don't be tempted to qualify it beforehand with a verbal laundry list of possible flaws. Learn to fight off that natural insecurity and present your work for what it is. Let it be judged on its own merits at face value, then critique it afterward with feedback from the group.

202
Accept the invitation.

Just go! Go visit your Peace Corps friend volunteering in Guatemala; go wear a fancy dress to the Daytime Emmys; go chat with the boys at the Ghanaian Soccer Academy benefit. When you get an invitation to do something out of the ordinary, see it as a little microcosm of life's possibilities and say "yes," even if you're tired, nervous, or uncertain. At least when you're older, you'll be able to reflect on your adventures, instead of regretting shiny bubbles of opportunity that floated away while you were moored to the couch.

203

Return your shopping cart.

Abandoning your shopping cart in the
middle of the parking lot implies a sense
of entitlement. Someone has to put it away;
that someone should be you.

204

Be candid.

Use language that is free from subterfuge to
render opinions that are frank, outspoken, and
sincere. Choose appropriate moments to do
so and strive to be impartial and unreserved. If
you can develop consistency and compassion
in this regard, you will be known as a trusted
friend and valued confidant. Simultaneously,
you will be cultivating an honest and forthright
relationship with the observations and emotions
roiling about in your own head.

205

**If you rely on popular culture definitions
of love, you will live in a state of
constant disappointment.**

Forget the love you see in screenplays
and on sitcoms; your life is more tangled, more
interesting, and, frankly, much longer
than a movie.

Having a Coke with you

    is even more fun than going to San Sebastian, Irún, Hendaye, Biarritz, Bayonne

    or being sick to my stomach on the Travesera de Gracia in Barcelona

    partly because in your orange shirt you look like a better happier St. Sebastian partly because of my love for you, partly because of your love for yoghurt

    partly because of the fluorescent orange tulips around the birches

    partly because of the secrecy our smiles take on before people and statuary

    it is hard to believe when I'm with you that there can be anything as still

    as solemn as unpleasantly definitive as statuary when right in front of it

    in the warm New York 4 o'clock light we are drifting back and forth

    between each other like a tree breathing through its spectacles

    and the portrait show seems to have no faces in it at all, just paint

    you suddenly wonder why in the world anyone ever did them

I look at you and I would rather look at you than all
the portraits in the world

except possibly for the *Polish Rider* occasionally
and anyway it's in the Frick

which thank heavens you haven't gone to yet so we
can go together the first time

and the fact that you move so beautifully more or
less takes care of Futurism

just as at home I never think of the *Nude
Descending a Staircase* or

at a rehearsal a single drawing of Leonardo or
Michelangelo that used to wow me

and what good does all the research of the Impres-
sionists do them

when they never got the right person to stand near
the tree when the sun sank

or for that matter Marino Marini when he didn't
pick the rider as carefully as the horse

it seems they were all cheated of some marvellous
experience

which is not going to go wasted on me which is
why I am telling you about it

       —Frank O'Hara

206
Visit a cave.
Caves are incredible!

207
Coloring your hair is an ongoing commitment.
Think long and hard before you begin dyeing your hair—once you start it's difficult to go back. A lot of upkeep is required to ensure your roots aren't showing and the color hasn't faded; a lot of energy is spent agonizing over the most flattering shade and complementary tone. One day you may realize that you've spent endless hours and countless dollars in the salon chair just trying to recapture the beautiful hair color you were born with.

208
Your sexuality is not a bargaining chip in the negotiation of life.
Don't trade on it; it is something specifically and only yours to explore and enjoy with someone you love. If you treat it as anything more or anything less, you're just gambling away your shot at true intimacy in pursuit of a false sense of self worth.

209
If you test people, they may fail.
Friendship, love, and family don't hinge on any single success or failure; you would do yourself a disservice to administer litmus tests to things as labyrinthine as love and affection.

210
Acknowledge inequity.
Thomas Jefferson wrote in the Declaration of Independence, "All men are created equal." Today, we interpret "men" to mean "people," but at that time "men" was not intended to be inclusive of women, or even of men who were not white. Inequity existed two hundred years ago, and it still exists today. Don't let anyone tell you that everyone gets a fair shot. Be sympathetic to the disadvantaged and work hard to include them.

211
Stop when it's done.
With any creative pursuit, learning when to stop is part of the challenge; this type of editing can be what separates ordinary from excellent. It's very easy to make an oil painting muddy, an essay overcomplicated, or a stir-fry mushy by not realizing when the work is complete.

212
Remember that most fairy tales were written by men.

Some of the greatest writers of children's fables were male: the Brothers Grimm, Hans Christian Andersen, even Walt Disney. You are not a tiny princess awaiting rescue by a valiant man, a symbol of frailty and naïveté, or the punch line in a morality tale. The women in those stories were crafted by a different sex at a different time for a different audience; these days you slay the dragon yourself.

213
Create a sense of family wherever you are.

Find people to love and love them unconditionally.

214
Try not to wait eagerly for people to finish their stories just so you can tell your own versions that more directly involve you.

215
Pursue more than just the things you are good at.

You will be told at a young age what your talents are. Enjoy the compliments, but don't accept them at face value. You don't want to walk a narrow path; attempt things you aren't comfortable with and uncover skills or proclivities you didn't know you possessed.

216
When wearing a dress or skirt, the hem should fall below the tips of your fingers when your arms hang straight at your sides.

217
Having good taste and being a good person are not the same thing.

218
You can't base the big decisions in your life on what you think will make other people happy.

It never works anyway.

219
Everyone is a hypocrite.
Hypocrisy is not the blanket failure it's made out
to be; we all act in ways that conflict with the
image we want to reflect or the values we want
to embody. Try not to pigeonhole people with
expectations; be forgiving of this inconsistency,
both in yourself and in others.

220
**If you are passionate about a craft, invest
in the best equipment you can afford.**
Whether in photography, making music,
woodworking, or cooking, the right equipment
makes a difference in the finished quality of your
work. What is money for if not to feed your
passions? Invest in your talent.

221
You don't need the extended warranty.

222

If love were enough, no one would ever die.
Yet death is inevitable. Mourning invites magical
thinking; you may wonder what you might have
done differently to alter what has happened,
whether a person would still be alive if you had
only loved better or more. Your love can't keep
death at bay, my daughter. But it can comfort
you. There is nothing more I can say about
grieving; you just grieve.

Big Band, Slow Dance
Were you close? I'm asked, as if grief
Would sting less deeply were we friends
As well as son and father. Further apart
Two men could never meet, though blood bends

Through arteries, veins and capillaries
Summoned into Presence by his pleasure.
Oh that I could have grown more slowly—
Remember being held, and cradled like treasure.
                                    —Bill Mohr

People will fail.

The unfortunate reality is that people will fail you, and you will experience what broken trust does to relationships. I hope that as a consequence, you learn the true value of the faith people place in you. Be worthy of it.

Lies About Love

We are all liars, because
the truth of yesterday becomes a lie tomorrow,
whereas letters are fixed,
and we live by the letter of truth.
The love I feel for my friend, this year,
is different from the love I felt last year.
If it were not so, it would be a lie.
Yet we reiterate love! love! love!
as if it were a coin with fixed value
instead of a flower that dies, and opens a different bud.

—D. H. Lawrence

224
Vanity license plates are for vain people.

225
You will get good at anything you practice.
Everything gets easier the more you do it, good
or bad, so choose your habits wisely.

226
Leave a decent tip.
People who work for tips earn their livelihoods
at your mercy. A tip is not a tool to coerce the
server or hairstylist to indulge your whims; it's
simply the currency of service jobs. An adequate
job requires a standard tip, and outstanding
service should be rewarded with a bigger one.
Don't think of a tip as a supplemental cost; it is
as integral to your purchase as the tax you pay.
This is something you will really embrace once
you have the opportunity to slave away in a
tip-earning position. Doing that job will teach
you a genuine respect for service workers,
and to tip generously.

227
Get in a boat and go out to sea.

Go far enough that you see only water on one endless horizon. Turn the engines off. Listen to the ocean. Grasp the magnitude of this planet.

228
When your tax bill goes up, revel in all the libraries, schools, and roads you are helping to maintain.

And really, a higher tax bill means you've made more money. Take pride in that and in your contribution to the civil services those taxes pay for.

229
When you smile you are radiant!

You are luminous and resplendent. You are rapturous and incandescent.

230
Politics truly can be a noble profession.

Genuine politics—even politics worthy of the name—
the only politics I am willing to devote myself to—is
simply a matter of serving those around us: serving
the community and serving those who will come after
us. Its deepest roots are moral because it is a responsibility expressed through action, to and for the whole.

—Václav Havel

231
Come home.

Don't stay away from home for too long,
if only because my heart breaks a little every
week we spend apart.

232
You can tell me your secrets.

If you are privy to someone else's secret, I advise
you to keep it in confidence. But if you have a
secret that's gnawing you from the inside out,
you can unload it onto me. I promise never to
judge you, to keep your secret locked in the
vault, and to respect your decision if you choose
not to share it with me at all.

233
You are more than a footnote in someone else's story.

Don't be "the other woman." She's always a quick side note in the great saga of another couple's love. Cast yourself as the lead in your own life, please.

234
Take pride in your work.

People will repeatedly tell you that to be truly happy, you must find a job that you *love*. I sincerely hope that you do. But in case you have to take a less-than-ideal position to pay the bills, there are some things you should know. Avoid any job that you find morally objectionable—you can't reconcile your values with tasks you find repugnant. But you can earn rewards from a job that you find only mildly tolerable. When you are presented with a challenge and use your skills to meet it, you will feel accomplished, regardless of the task. That feeling is universally valid and undeniably admirable; embracing it will make work a more rewarding experience in the day to day, even if it doesn't feed your soul.

235

There is that moment in an argument when you realize you're wrong.

At that point, stop arguing.

236

Wanting to change the world isn't naive; it's normal.

I hope you are able to fend off cynicism as long as possible to keep your youthful passion sincere and viable.

237

Consider what constitutes a good life.

Your assumptions about this will change as you age. That's normal. A picket fence lifestyle that once seemed torturously confining might one day seem comfortably secure; a personality that once struck you as overly emotional may grow sympathetic. What you think you want to have or be at any given moment isn't really important; what matters is that you are present in your own life, considering it and shaping it with the force of your will.

238
Where there's smoke there's fire.

When there are facts that you don't want to
face, it's tempting to rationalize them away and
avoid the truth. This type of self-deception
only mires you deeper in the muck.
Trust your instincts: Things are usually exactly
what they seem to be.

239
Anything you chase after runs.

240
Make yourself useful.

Get off your butt and lend a hand. Providing
active service helps others and makes your life
richer. Clear the table, water the plants, cook
dinner, babysit: I can't explain exactly why,
but I promise that you will feel incrementally
better about yourself and your life every
single time you get up and do something
for someone else.

241

Your future together is not a great subject to discuss on a first date.

242

Plan your first pregnancy.

It's simple to avoid an unplanned pregnancy: You use birth control or you don't have sex. If you feel uncomfortable talking to your partner about birth control, then you simply aren't ready to have a sexual relationship (or a baby) yet. That's okay; there is plenty of time for that later.

243

The Grand Canyon is as amazing as everyone says it is.

244

If you don't have money to buy an extravagant gift for someone special, bake!

245

**Summer camp will always be among
your best memories.**

Dances, campfires, and archery: It's
independence without responsibilities.

246

**If you have to tell someone no,
do it in person.**

I learned this from a business associate,
but it's a good rule of thumb for personal
interactions as well.

247

Know how to spot charlatans.

Bombastic claims and grandiose promises are
clear signs of hucksterism. Don't allow yourself
to be sucked into schemes designed to
separate you from your money by playing
on your emotions.

248
Discipline in your mind;
extravagance in your heart.

Every Time I Kiss You
Every time I kiss you
After a long separation
I feel
I am putting a hurried love letter
In a red mailbox.

—Nizar Qabbani

249
Stay conscious of your cholesterol.
Cholesterol is a white soapy substance found in
the tissues of humans and other animals. HDL
cholesterol is helpful to your body; it produces
cell membranes and some of your hormones.
LDL cholesterol can be unhealthy for you. If too
much of it collects on the walls of your arteries,
it will interfere with the flow of blood to your
heart and brain, which could lead to a heart
attack or stroke. To avoid this problem,
choose whole grains and foods with less
saturated fat and more fiber.

250

Hold the door open.

Be the person who holds the door open, even if you have to stand there too long, and no one nods in acknowledgment. Be satisfied with the fact that you've extended a small gesture of helpfulness to strangers.

251

Never pass up a hayride, fresh cow milk, or conversation with a farmer.

You will have many opportunities to savor these experiences at the family farm.

252

Before you leave for an international trip, scan your passport and e-mail it to yourself.

It's much easier to replace a lost passport when you have an accessible copy. You could also upload it to the Web somewhere.

253

Pay no attention to the line of impossibility.

Subconscious belief that there is a line you cannot cross—a line that separates the realistic from the impossible—is what keeps talented people from achieving success. If you want to write the great American novel, star in a Tom Stoppard play, or be point guard for the Sparks, just research the usual steps needed to do those things, then embark upon the journey. Whether you succeed or not will be based on your talent, not your drive; that's respectable.

254

Imagine your father seeing that picture of you.

Pictures are easily transmitted and recorded for posterity. The consequences of allowing yourself to be captured in a compromising light might not be apparent to you now, but they will be one day. The best advice I can give you is to avoid being snapped doing anything you wouldn't want your father to see.

255
You are not a cheater.
The way you prove this is by not cheating on anything or anyone. There's no excuse for it.

256
A nickname should be a term of endearment, not an insult.
If you get burdened with a nickname you don't like, kindly ask the name-caller to stop it. If you give someone else a nickname, base it on something positive.

257
Nothing can ruin your life like drugs.
I want to be honest with you, because there
is a lot of fear mongering clouding the choices
you are going to face. I'll admit it's a fact that
some people are able to use drugs without
fundamentally destroying their lives; however,
you must assume that you are not one of them.
You can't know how you will react to various
drugs unless you try them, but the catch is that
if you're part of the majority who can't control
their usage, trying drugs will send you down
a spiral from which it will be all but impossible
to recover. Every drug user alters his or her
life's potential; drugs rob you of ambition and
disconnect you from your identity. This is one of
the very few lessons that I hope you do not have
to learn through experience. The thought of
your tiny perfection being usurped by chemical
addiction is too much for me to bear.

258

Never push a person off a boat.

Pushing someone into a pool is okay,
but only the deep end.

259

Try to speak the local language.

I have found that people appreciate even the
clumsiest attempts at speaking their native
language; it shows respect. Aside from ordinary
greetings and pleasantries, these phrases are
quite convenient to know: If traveling for work,
"Can I get a receipt, please?" If traveling with
smokers, "May we have an ashtray?" And, of
course, "I'm sorry, I don't speak French/Turkish/
Russian/Japanese."

260

Sometimes you have to cry it out.

A good crying jag can be cathartic. It's a girl
thing. Just don't do it at work.

261
Look people in the eye.
It can be uncomfortable, but do it anyway.

262
The person who asked for the date is generally expected to foot the bill.
But you should always offer to contribute.

263
Accept chivalry.
When your father and I started dating, I was shocked by the way he held every door for me and grasped my hand when I stepped off a low curb. Despite being secretly smitten by these gestures, in my self-righteous youth, I responded with ridiculous assertions that I could *do it myself*. I kept up this charade until the day he bluntly told me to lay off. He knew I was perfectly capable of the simple task of opening a door; he just wanted to do it for me! Then and now, I revel in your father's dedication to old-fashioned chivalry: He still walks to the

passenger side of the car to open the door for me; he refuses to allow me to carry heavy things; and he insists that I wrap myself in his coat, even though I knew it would be a cold night and left my warm jacket at home because it didn't coordinate with my dress. This is what's known as gallantry. Know that you aren't entitled to it, and you can't expect it, but in those rare cases when you find it beating down your door, embrace it! Also, thank your father for showing you how it's done.

264
People can change, but you can't change them.

265
You don't have to stick to the recipe.
Unless you are baking—then, stick to the recipe.

266
At least try.
Whether it's tasting a new food, trying a new
sport, or venturing to a new place, you won't
know how you really feel about it until
you give it a shot.

267
**Mother's Day is more than a
"Hallmark holiday."**
You won't really appreciate this until you
become a mother yourself.

268
**You will want some things that
you will not get.**
You don't get everything you want in life.
That's all there is to say about that.

269
Always treat a gun like it's loaded.
It's the cardinal rule of gun handling: Never point
a gun, loaded or not, at anyone.

270
Support local charities.
Give some of your money and some of your time to nonprofit groups. I recommend choosing a local organization like a shelter or museum so you can see the direct benefit of your participation, rather than a celebrity-supported cause—they already get plenty of attention.

271
Think about the time zone before you dial.
I can't tell you how many innocent British husbands I've awakened at ungodly hours to answer my calls from the United States. Their wives remind me, so I remind you, to check the time before calling overseas.

272
Visit Fenway Park, Wrigley Field, and Dodger Stadium.
They won't be around much longer; there's nothing like a day at a legendary ballpark.

273
Your rights are both sacred and fragile.
Know that some of those responsible for
protecting your rights are doing just that, but
some are angling to undo them. Be aware of
this when voting for politicians and interacting
with the police. You counterbalance this kind of
power by knowing your rights.

274
Know your local government.
Know the names of the people who represent
you in government, as well as their positions on
pertinent issues. Write to them. If you are lucky
enough to be represented by a congressperson
you respect and admire, donate money to
his or her campaign.

Get the assistant on your team.
In business it always helps to befriend the
executive assistant; he or she holds a lot of sway
behind the scenes. Make sure the assistant who
orders lunch for your conference gets a plate
of food, include him or her in as many business
decisions as reasonably possible, and remember
his or her birthday. These are kind gestures
with obvious benefits: If the assistant likes you,
chances are, the boss will like you.

276

Chin out and down.
This is the trick to avoiding a double chin in
photographs. You want to stretch your neck up
and out to a slightly unnatural degree (you'll feel
like a giraffe), then tilt your chin downward.

277

Visit Washington, D.C.
Your father and I will take you there after you
learn to read and write. It's important that you
know our capital and feel the energy of your
government at work.

College is a time to study your passions.

If I understood then what I know now—
that college is the best opportunity to study
everything and anything that sparks your
interest, rather than just a way to prepare
for a career—I would've approached it
very differently. You will never again have
the opportunity to spend such quality time
immersed in pursuits that fascinate you. The
day will come that you are focused on a single
vocation; college is not that day. Discover
your interests and take advantage of the
atmosphere of scholarly curiosity.

Respect the law, but don't be afraid to fight it.

Obey laws even when they are unjust. Doing
so is part of the social contract that allows us to
live communally and without fear. Fight unjust
laws through peaceful resistance and political
activism. Look to Jane Addams, Mohandas
Gandhi, Martin Luther King Jr., and
Bella Abzug, among others.

280

The first stall is always the cleanest.

I've heard that people half-consciously assume
that the first stall in a public restroom is dirty
and consequently skip it, so it actually
remains more sanitary.

281

**If your clothes sit in the dryer too long,
they'll get wrinkled and then you'll
have to iron them.**

282

Say "Bless you" when people sneeze.

Inject a little jolt of courtesy into the day.

283

Learn to swim.

Swimming isn't an innate human skill.
You should practice it for your own safety and
because swimming is fun.

284
Conserve water in every little way that you can.

When you see how people live when they do not have access to free-flowing clean water, your heart will break. The reality that water is a finite resource will be seared into your brain. Grow water-conserving plants, turn the faucet off while brushing your teeth, install a shut-off nozzle on your hose, be cognizant of your individual impact on this global problem.

285
Never park in the handicapped spot.

These spots are reserved for people who have difficulty moving from place to place because of a disability. It is a gross act of selfishness to rob someone of this small convenience. For as long as your body works as it should, savor that fact while you walk from farther away!

286
Use serif fonts for your printed work.
Serif fonts have little flourishes on the ends of
the letters while sans-serif fonts do not (*"sans"*
means "without" in French). Sans-serif fonts
are cleaner and more modern, but the flourishes
make serif letters easier for the eye to distinguish
on paper. This isn't a hard and fast rule, but for
homework and manuscripts, it's good to know.

287
**Always pay taxes on the money you earn,
even if it wasn't totally above board.**
That's how they got Capone.

288
Have a little black dress.
One you can dress up or down so it's always
appropriate; one that makes you feel beautiful
whenever you wear it.

289

Read Thomas Pynchon, Don DeLillo, and Vladimir Nabokov.

This is your father's literary canon; reading it will help you understand him.

290

If it's not a problem, don't make it a problem.

This is usually one of those things you don't realize you're doing until you've gone and done it, but try to stop yourself anyway.

291

If you meet people knowledgeable about a subject you're interested in, offer to take them out to lunch.

People generally love to share both their expertise and a meal.

292
Befriend the delivery person.
I don't know why, but all the delivery people I
have gotten to know are very interesting. Also, if
you make friends with them, it is safe to assume
your items will be handled with extra care.

293
Strive for authenticity.
Try to know and reflect your best self. Aiming for
anything else is simply diversion, or else delusion.

294
The key to a good scrambled egg is a
tablespoon of milk and whisking
until you see bubbles.

295
Do not abide systemic human suffering.

Washing one's hands of the conflict between the
powerful and the powerless means to side with the
powerful, not to be neutral.
                                        —Paulo Freire

There is "cheesy" and there is "classic."

If a romantic gesture is forced, it will seem corny. But when offered with sincerity, flower arrangements are beautiful gifts of affection, sunset walks are timeless memories, and home-cooked meals are evidence of kindly devotion. Don't shy away from romance; embrace tradition while rejecting symbolism for symbolism's sake.

In Paris with You

Don't talk to me of love. I've had an earful
And I get tearful when I've downed a drink or two.
I'm one of your talking wounded.
I'm a hostage. I'm marooned.
But I'm in Paris with you.
Yes I'm angry at the way I've been bamboozled
And resentful at the mess I've been through.
I admit I'm on the rebound
And I don't care where are we bound.

I'm in Paris with you.
Do you mind if we do not go to the Louvre
If we say sod off to sodding Notre Dame,
If we skip the Champs Elysées
And remain here in this sleazy
Old hotel room
Doing this and that
To what and whom
Learning who you are,
Learning what I am.
Don't talk to me of love. Let's talk of Paris,
The little bit of Paris in our view.
There's that crack across the ceiling
And the hotel walls are peeling
And I'm in Paris with you.
Don't talk to me of love. Let's talk of Paris.
I'm in Paris with the slightest thing you do.
I'm in Paris with your eyes, your mouth,
I'm in Paris with . . . all points south.
Am I embarrassing you?
I'm in Paris with you.

—James Fenton

Diamonds may be a symbol of love, but they are also a retail product.

Diamonds have no intrinsic value; they are worth only as much as you believe they are. The belief that sparkly stones and everlasting romantic commitment are necessarily correlated can create a quandary when partners share limitless love but only limited money. So please recognize that the size, cut, weight, and clarity of a diamond bear zero relation to the love someone has for you.

The waiting is the hardest part.

Patience is a challenge (at least for me). Life is full of inevitable waits: standing in line, longing to hear the phone ring, anticipating a baby's birth, watching the figurative horizon for your ship to come in. If you can find a way to deal with the waiting—some method of building your capacity to endure—you will save yourself accumulated years of pointless agitation. And if you do find a way, please teach it to me.

299

**Walking away from oil on the stove
is a guaranteed disaster.**

300

Share.

Everything is enhanced through
communal experience.

301

Handling money is simple.

Save some, spend some, and give some
away. Learn the basics of investing and asset
allocation, be conscientious about how much
you spend and what you spend it on, and
determine what percentage of your earnings
you will donate to charity. Reevaluate your
financial position at regular intervals and
adjust your distributions accordingly. If you
do this, you will feel secure and build a
healthy relationship with money.

302
It's never a good idea to stand on a rocking chair.

303
Regifting is tacky.

If you get a gift you don't like, it might be tempting to gift it to someone else. This is fraught with complications. There's a high chance that the giver and/or giftee will discover what you've done and be offended. But more important, if you didn't like the gift, it's just rude to give it to someone else; gifts are supposed to be thoughtful.

304
Stay out of jail.

I've been to jail, and the key thing I learned from the experience is that I don't want to go back. Losing your liberty inflicts a shocking dose of reality—you don't realize what a base animal need physical freedom is until you're deprived of it. You also don't need to experience

the indignity of using the toilet in front of thirty
people or watching a crowd of grown women
fight over your burrito. The good news is,
it's easy to stay out of jail—just don't
break any laws.

305
Buy something off the registry.
Unless the registry is chock-full of unreasonably
extravagant items, purchase at least one small
gift from it. Pick the most boring thing you
see (the diaper pail or the vacuum), and I
guarantee the receiver will be ecstatic that
you've given her something she really needs.
You can always supplement with a thoughtful
token of your own choosing.

306
Don't plagiarize.
Every original idea is built on the backs of
previous thinkers; therein lies the beauty of
history and collected wisdom. Simply cite those
who inspire you; never pass off their ideas or
words as your own.

307

If a book has been banned, you should probably read it.

Our government doesn't ban books anymore, but schools often do. This is usually due to dated and offensive slang or provocative themes that teachers or parents don't think you're ready for. I believe you are smart enough to grasp these intricacies, so go suck the marrow out of books such as *The Adventures of Huckleberry Finn, Brave New World, A Clockwork Orange, Go Ask Alice, The Grapes of Wrath, The Great Gatsby, The Handmaid's Tale, Heart of Darkness, I Know Why the Caged Bird Sings, Julie of the Wolves, Lolita, Lord of the Flies, Of Mice and Men, A Separate Peace, Their Eyes Were Watching God, To Kill a Mockingbird, A Wrinkle in Time.*

308

There's no need to curse excessively.

An occasional outburst isn't the end of the world, but ordinarily there are better ways to get your point across. Your great-great-grandfather would say that people who curse have small vocabularies.

309
Take care of your tools.
Clean your brushes and sharpen your chisels.
They are expensive to replace. It also shows
respect for your craft.

310
Really, don't talk with food in your mouth.
It's truly unpleasant to see someone's masticated
meal while they mumble!

311
Your father wants you to carry a knife.
I'm not so sure about this, but here is what
your dad has to say: "Carry a knife, and no, not
just for fending off would-be attackers. More
practically, the handiness of a pocketknife applies
to cutting loose strings, opening envelopes
and boxes, fishing out small items that fall in
between your car seat and the armrest, and so
many other simple, daily tasks it will surprise
you. Just remember to leave it at home
before going to the airport."

312
If you aren't in the mood to wash the dishes right away, at least rinse them off.
It will save you the aggravation of scrubbing at caked-on food.

313
Raising your voice won't make it any easier for someone who speaks a different language to understand what you're saying.

314
Use the good stuff.
There's no reason to hoard your possessions in anticipation of life's big events. Whip out your grandmother's jewelry, the fragile dishes, or your sexy lingerie to create little special occasions whenever you can.

315
Anticipation is 90 percent of the fun.
Savor it; don't peek!

316

Hire people who are smarter than you.

This is the mark of a good boss. Rid yourself
of insecurity; if your team shines, you shine.
Hiring people who are highly competent will
also teach you powerful skills: how to manage
intelligence and nurture creativity.

317

Women carry purses for a reason.

Preparedness. The necessities: your ID, your
telephone (charged), a credit card, a Band-Aid,
a tampon or two, a hair band, a mini-flashlight,
sunscreen, business cards, a pen, and your keys.

318

Choose the window seat.

There is nothing more awe-inspiring than a
rolling expanse of milk-white clouds as viewed
from the window seat of an airplane. It is
miraculous: You are flying.

319

A song is about one idea.

This is a helpful hint if you want to be a
songwriter; keep it simple and direct.

320

**The Internet is not the place to
diagnose your illness.**

Seriously, just go to the doctor.

321

If you need to remember it, write it down.

Something about the act of writing cements
things into memory.

322

**It's true what they say about
horizontal stripes.**

They really aren't flattering to any body type.

323

Jump-start your own car.

If the engine isn't cranking, your battery is probably dead. Grab your jumper cables and have someone with a working car pull up next to you. Start by attaching the red clamp to the positive terminal on the dead battery, then attach the other red clamp to the positive terminal on the good battery. Next take the black clamp and attach it to the negative terminal on your battery. The other black clamp should be attached to a clean metal surface, like a bolt or a bracket, on the good engine. Turn the good car on and let it run for a few minutes, and then start the dead car. Remove the clamps in the reverse order and let your car run for a good thirty minutes to give your battery a chance to recharge.

324

When the authorities tell you it's time, evacuate.

God forbid you ever find yourself in the path of a
natural disaster, but if that happens, don't be the
person stubbornly trying to rescue your house
with a garden hose long after the experts have
instructed you to leave; it's foolhardy and selfish.
The altruistic people who come to your rescue
risk death; they have families and friends and
lives whose value far outweighs that
of your home or belongings.

325

Befriend the new kid.

Once you've been the new kid you'll know
how important this is. Making friends is hard;
it's even harder if you don't know a soul.
Welcome someone into your circle, ask her a
question, invite her to sit with you. This type of
gesture will reward you throughout your life; I
remember being at a barbecue when I was ten

or eleven years old watching a new girl with her ear of corn looking around furtively for a circle to eat with. I invited her to sit with me. I don't know her now, nor do I remember her name, but I do remember being her friend on that day. It's a good memory.

326
Take the time to do it right the first time.
I always want to skip the endless measurements and planning at the beginning of a project and get right into the meat of it: the actual sawing, drilling, painting, or sewing. This approach rarely works in my favor, resulting in a poorly executed project or even worse—an unusable waste of materials, time, and energy. Consequently, I've learned to value the time spent preparing, and I hope to pass that on to you.

327
A woman is "pregnant" not "preggers."

328

**Ice is for acute swollen injuries;
heat is for chronic pain.**

Cold reduces swelling while heat stimulates
blood flow and relaxes muscles.

329

**Wear nude shades of underwear
with your white clothing.**

It's the only way to avoid panty lines.

330

Send a gift to your new coworkers.

When you accept a new position, it is
unexpectedly classy to send a gift the day before
you start work. Choose an edible gift that can
be shared by a group: a basket of cookies, a
box of delicious cupcakes, or a colorful fruit
arrangement. Have it delivered to your new
boss, and include a short card addressed
to your future colleagues expressing how
much you are looking forward to meeting
them all on Monday.

331
Spend as much time outdoors as you possibly can.

"Outside" is one of the most commonly used words in a baby's limited vocabulary. I imagine it's because there is something about being in the open air that you find nourishing. Remember to nurture that part of yourself.

332
Carve out the time to observe a comet!

When you are fifty-four years old, the elliptical orbit of Haley's comet will once again approach our sun, heating the dirty lump of gas and rock enough for us to see it. This is the sort of event that requires you to skip work, travel out of the city, and surrender yourself to the intangible importance of an astronomic occasion. I can't explain to you why exactly; I can only tell you that I missed it when I was eight, and I long to see it with you when I am eighty-four.

333
Take naps.
For most of your life, you will feel slightly tired unless you can learn to nap as an adult like you did as a child.

334
Curiosity didn't kill any cats.
I once asked your dad a stupid question: Did he think he was smarter than me? I will always remember what he said, and how it touched me. He thoughtfully scrunched his brow and looked slightly to the left as he always does, then slowly explained: "We are equally knowledgeable, but while I'm satisfied with what I know, you are always curious. That's why I love you."

335
Marry someone like your father.
If you do get married, you can't go wrong if you choose someone like your dad: kind, warm, affectionate, intelligent, funny, and, most important, madly in love with you.

336
Your grandfather reminds you that sunshine and rain are both needed to grow.

He is both a farmer and an engineer who specializes in weather sciences, so I think this is particularly wise.

337
You are going to get old.

It's okay. It's more than okay. One day you'll pray you have the chance to stay that long.

The Act
There were the roses, in the rain.
Don't cut them, I pleaded.
They won't last, she said.
But they're so beautiful
where they are.
Agh, we were all beautiful once, she said,
and cut them and gave them to me
in my hand.

— William Carlos Williams

338

Raw and ragged are the sensations of inspiration.

When you are worn, when you are battered, when you feel worse for wear, find a way to look beyond these temporary illusions to the grand vision of your life. These feelings are what feed you; they are the motivation underlying your future greatness, exposed for you to examine.

339

There are a few important pieces of wedding-day wisdom.

If you decide to have a wedding, keep these time-tested nuggets in mind on the big day: Remember to eat; wear comfortable shoes and underwear; focus on what it is really about (no one cares if the tablecloths are the wrong shade of yellow); and have sex that night. That last one is harder than it sounds.

340
You can't set out to make a masterpiece.
There will be too much pressure to ever begin.
Create for the sake of creating and believe the
masterpiece will eventually reveal itself. If you
can't approach it that way, then you don't really
enjoy the work, and if you don't really enjoy it,
you can't create a magnum opus anyway.

341
**Sometimes you just have to take
the bad news.**
There will be good news soon enough.

342
Just ask.
People are generally very helpful if you just ask.
Some examples: When checking into a hotel, if
you ask for a better room, they will often give
it to you. If you're too cold, ask and usually the
hostess will turn the air-conditioning down. If
you need help moving your couch, ask a few
friends, and someone will likely oblige.

343
Take yourself on dates.
A delicious restaurant, a visit to the museum, a matinee—you are your own best company.

344
Consider it material.
When absurd things happen, try to look at the experience as good material for storytelling over a glass of wine with friends rather than dwelling on the negative aspects. What could be funnier than dropping a gourmet chicken down the stairs or cleaning baby poop out of bath toys? Material.

345
Learn how to fold a fitted sheet.
You're going to have fitted sheets; you might as well know how to fold one:

Fold it in half lengthwise and line up the corners at the seams. Flip the corners over so the elastic part is inward and you've created little pockets. Fold it into thirds widthwise, bringing the sides to the center, then do the same lengthwise. You should have a relatively flat and square package that won't make you crazy when you see it on the shelf.

346
Often the answer will manifest itself.
Redirect your focus from fixing what's wrong to opening yourself up. Look for the signs instead of the solutions—they might lead you to the conclusion you're seeking.

347
Recognize a distinction without a difference.
In the course of an argument, whether friendly or heated, it often happens that one party attempts to use different wording to advance a previously refuted assertion. The claim *sounds* new, but the substance is the same. If you are losing a debate, you might be tempted to recycle old arguments; this is a form of sophistry you should work hard to avoid.

348
Pack a bathing suit.
You never know when the opportunity to swim might present itself.

349

Every time you describe your good deed, you diminish it a little bit.

If you find yourself seeking credit for gestures of decency and goodwill, it is time to evaluate your intentions. Acknowledgment is not the real reward for kindness.

350

If there are three or more instructional signs, just park somewhere else.

Three signs guarantee a ticket; trust me on this one.

351

Giving and receiving constructive criticism are skills you should practice.

Criticism can be a positive experience, but egos are delicate and easily damaged. The cardinal rule of giving criticism is to address the work or action, not the character or personality. Start with honest compliments to cushion the blow and provide suggested solutions to any problem you see. When receiving criticism, call on your reserves of humility. Remember that constructive criticism is a gift of time and attention, and be grateful for it.

352

We communicate through a system of symbols.

Speech, body language, written words. These symbols are our imperfect attempts to connect with one another and feel less alone.
Be forgiving of their limitations.

353

Rain is romantic.

Maybe I believe this only because it doesn't rain much where we live, but I think the sound and smell reconnect you to your animal self. Bask in it.

354

Dance with anyone who asks.

355
If you want a different life, you have to make a different life.

They always say time changes things, but you actually have to change them yourself.

—Andy Warhol

356
Develop your sense of situational awareness.

Be cognizant of the activity going on around you; locate your position in the physical and emotional landscape.

357
Bypass the second cheapest wine on the list.

Restaurateurs know that people order the second least expensive wine so as not to appear cheap; therefore, this wine carries the highest markup. Order the wine you want, knowing the least expensive and most expensive bottles are usually the best value.

358

**It's a good parlor trick to be an
encyclopedia of acronyms.**

Your dad thinks of them as tiny hidden
dictionaries waiting to be opened—decoder
rings for complex subjects like NASA or laser.

359

**The proper way to hold a hammer
is at the end.**

Hammering a nail is a basic mechanical
operation; the hammer is designed to be the
length it is because it creates the most efficient
fulcrum for transmitting force from your
arm to the nail.

360
Engage your senses.
We construct our impressions of the world
through five concrete means: sight, taste, touch,
sound, and smell. Pause to remind yourself
that your perception is entwined with these
primal information-gathering tools. Feed them
something rich: Look at something beautiful; eat
something delicious; touch something soft; listen
to something soothing; smell something sweet.
Small adjustments in your environment can
create powerful changes in your mood.

361
**To regain control of your car in a skid,
turn the steering wheel in the
direction you're going.**
It's counterintuitive but it works.

362
Chronic tardiness is a form of arrogance.
Unless you are dying, your time is not more
valuable than anyone else's.

363
Find your tribe.
You will always exist as a member of two circles:
the family you were given and the friends that
you make. You only have power over the latter,
so be discriminating. Give everything you can
to those who are worthy; quietly jettison those
who don't replenish you.

364
You are the sole owner of your values.
Your dad and I have done our best to instill in
you a sense of what we believe is important,
but we are not you. You must examine
your own relationships—with yourself,
with us, with the world at large—and use the
information gleaned to determine what
you need to find contentment.

365
Foster your curiosity about the unknown.

The most beautiful thing we can experience is the mysterious. It is the source of all true art and all science. He to whom this emotion is a stranger, who can no longer pause to wonder and stand rapt in awe, is as good as dead: His eyes are closed.

—Albert Einstein

366
Being intelligent, beautiful, wealthy, talented, witty, or powerful is meaningless if you are not also kind.

367
Only borrow money from a bank.

Also, if you lend money to friends, be sure that it's money you don't need back; call it a loan, but consider it a gift.

The holy passion of Friendship is of so sweet and steady and loyal and enduring a nature that it will last through a whole lifetime, if not asked to lend money.

—Mark Twain

You are looking for someone who is out there looking for you.

Maybe you played together on the monkey bars
in elementary school. Or maybe you will both
change planes on a cloudy day in Zurich, passing
each other on the concourse, never to meet. I'm
not proposing that you spend your life waiting
for this mysterious soul mate to materialize;
I'm telling you that as you imagine your perfect
match, there is a person out there imagining
someone just like you.

Morning at Last: There in the Snow
Morning at last: there in the snow
Your small blunt footprints come and go.
Night has left no more to show,
Not the candle, the half-drunk wine,
Or touching joy: only this sign
Of your life walking into mine.
But when they vanish with the rain
What morning woke to will remain
Whether as happiness or pain.

—Philip Larkin

369

Be levelheaded when it comes to sales.

If you really want something but can't afford it,
wait and hope it goes on sale. If you really want
something and can afford it, go ahead and buy
it. It also makes sense to shop around for the
best price on a specific item. But don't head to
every sale you hear about and start thumbing
through the racks with your coupons convincing
yourself you need things just because they are
discounted. People who do that have a lot of
useless stuff and a lot less money.

370

Revel and make merry.

Drink wine. This is life eternal. This is all that youth
will give you. It is the season for wine, roses, and
drunken friends. Be happy for this moment. This
moment is your life.

—Omar Khayyám

371
It is possible to be both pretty and smart.
They don't always go together, certainly, but one thing does not preclude the other. This goes for you and also for people you meet.

372
Clutter in your house is clutter in your brain.
The contents of your shelter reflect the content of your life. On some level, regardless of your income or your style, the way you keep your home is a representation of the way you address your world; curate it for maximum efficiency and enjoyment.

373
Humility will bring you closer to truth.

374
If you think it needs a second coat of paint, it does.
Go ahead and do it while the paint and brush are out.

375

If you skip family gatherings you'll regret it when you're older.

Family get-togethers can be stressful and worrisome; I get that. But go anyway. You will eventually forgive your relatives the annoying outbursts, lapses in judgment, and unwitting alienation they may have inflicted. One day, those frustrations will give way to cozy familial love, and you will wish you'd enjoyed more time together before they were gone forever.

376

An infinite number of things can add up to one finite thing.

The concept of limits, like other concepts that come out of calculus, is a basic tool for understanding many important things in everyday experience: that boundaries can exist, even around an infinite number of things; that everything can be broken into smaller components; that for many things, comprehending the true shape requires an understanding of the components, possibly down to the level of the infinitely small; and that the farther we are from such a detailed understanding, the more crude our approximation of the true shape.

377

When you have people over for dinner, plan on a balance of foods you can make ahead of time and foods that need your attention at the last moment.

378

Keep your bedroom a haven of peacefulness.

Watch television on the couch, eat food at the table, do work at the desk, and renew yourself in the bed.

379

You don't have to pick the flowers to enjoy them.

Afternoon on a Hill

I will be the gladdest thing
        Under the sun!
I will touch a hundred flowers
        And not pick one.

I will look at cliffs and clouds
        With quiet eyes.
Watch the wind bow down the grass.
        And the grass rise.

And when lights begin to show
        Up from the town,
I will mark which must be mine.
        And then start down!

                —Edna St. Vincent Millay

380

**Halloween costumes
should be scary, not sexy.**

People who dress up as "sexy nurses" or "hot
devils" on Halloween are out of touch with
their own sexuality, and they use the holiday to
explore it. Besides the general sadness of that,
it's not in the spirit of the day. Halloween is
about acknowledging and having fun with our
collective fears, so be scary.

381

**Go ahead and frown if you need to.
Your face won't freeze that way.**

382

**When "Here Comes the Sun"
comes on the radio, smile.**

This song was playing when I walked down the
aisle to marry your dad. You are our sun.

383
Doing things inspires doing more and greater things.

Doing nothing breeds inertia. When you do anything at all, no matter how insignificant, you begin to create a sphere of action and intention that expands around you.

384
The answer to the question "Is it art?" is yes.

It's one human being's intention that makes it art. It is the artist's attempt to communicate with you. Whether you appreciate or enjoy it is irrelevant to its standing as art.

385
Instead of spending money on premade salad dressing, spend it on a good vinegar wardrobe.

Red wine, balsamic, rice, and apple cider vinegar are all good, versatile starters. Champagne vinegar and fruit vinegars are fun additions. A good oil-to-vinegar ratio is three to one.

386
Find a sport that you love.
Engage in it even after you graduate from school. The camaraderie is enjoyable, but as you age and your priorities shift, it's the habit you've created that will prove invaluable.

387
There's often more completeness in being one than in being two.
You'll understand this better when you've been on your own for a while.

388
When you can't sleep because your head is filled with anxious thoughts, cook an imaginary meal.
That works for me. You might need to decorate a house or create a spreadsheet. Go through the motions of something you like doing that can be done differently every time, and next thing you know, it will be morning.

389

The book *is* better than the movie.

When you read a novel you are engaging your
own imagination rather than observing someone
else's interpretation.

390

**Chemistry is the reason some people are
right on paper and wrong in person.**

It's a variable you can't predict or change.

391

**Be the person who reacts in a
crowd of strangers.**

What I mean is this: Don't let your position
in a group of nameless faces numb you to
your responsibilities. If a stranger is choking, if
you witness a car accident, if you see a child
wandering alone—don't assume someone
else will take charge. Be the one who drops
everything to help.

392

If you chase after prestige, you won't be satisfied with what you catch.

Seeking status is an easy trap to fall into when considering a car, a school, a career, or even a mate. Know that when you make a choice based on this criterion, you embrace perception over reality. You'll be rewarded with fleeting admiration; you'll be left to live with your compromise.

Second Fig
Safe upon the solid rock the ugly houses stand:
Come and see my shining palace built upon the sand!
—Edna St. Vincent Millay

393

Procrastination is your enemy.

We all do it, and we all regret it. The only way to avoid procrastinating is to recognize that moment when you decide that a task can wait and consciously change the decision. You won't always succeed, but being aware of your own responsibility for the choice will alleviate a good portion of stress.

394
Vaccinate your children.
Vaccination of your children not only protects
them against disease, it protects your entire
community and is therefore part of your
responsibility as a member of society.

395
You don't have as much time as you think.
It all goes by so quickly, daughter. You can't
fathom it. If you could, you would collapse from
the weight of it—the unbearable comprehension
of the brevity of your time on earth. You will
sadly discover that lives end in inconceivable
ways and at puzzling times. At certain
moments, you will grasp the delicateness
of your life. Let them weigh on you;
let them change you.

396
Hydrate.
Drink water. It's good for your skin, it's
delicious, and you will feel a teensy bit better
every time you do it.

397
Have a best friend.
Show your guts to one person outside of your family and romances. Learn to love and be loved, learn to understand and be understood, learn to choose and be chosen.

398
The most effective way to handle someone who is yelling at you is to lower your own voice below normal talking volume.

399
Read the manual.
Technology should not baffle you.

400
When fresh flowers start to wilt, cut their stems and put them in tiny vases.

401
Plan your escape route.
When driving, give yourself space on all sides. When in a large building, know where the stairwells are located. When mired in a job you don't like, make connections. Getting out is as important as getting in.

402
In Monopoly, always buy railroads; never buy utilities.

403
The sun rises in the east and sets in the west.
This will help you get your bearings when you're lost.

404
Attack the soft parts.
Your father fears that one day a man who's
physically stronger than you may overpower
you. If this happens, he advises you to assault
the man's soft parts: gouge his eyes, clap his
ears, chop his throat, punch his stomach, and
kick his groin. I've never done it, and it sounds
unpleasant, but it was really important
to him that I tell you.

405
Frequent your local merchants.
Local businesses are your friends and neighbors.
As they go, so goes your community.

406
Go to the aquarium.
There's a lot happening underwater, and you
should get a look.

407
Keep your passport current.
You never know where the day might take you.

408
Your friends need your help most during the first months of motherhood.
Offering to hold the baby while she naps is the single best thing you can do for a new mom; it may seem awkward, but it is what she really wants to do. Ask her if she has showered and eaten, prepare her a meal, and make sure she has a glass of water if she's breastfeeding. If she's a close friend, do a load of laundry and take out the trash. If you are visiting from out of town, stay in a hotel. If you are visiting for a week or an hour, do not expect to be entertained. And above all else, take an interest in the child; tell her how beautiful her baby is.

409
Read the labels on the food you eat.
It's okay to eat some processed food, just be wary of the ones with labels listing various names for added sugars, high sodium content, or a plethora of words you can't pronounce.

410
Be assertive.
People who don't learn to assert themselves are left to stew on their frustrations, and they tend to find indirect ways to express these resentments. The frustrations manifest themselves as stubbornness, procrastination, a sense of victimization, and general pessimism. If you don't learn to assert yourself, you may become so mired in resentment that you'll never find any satisfaction.

411
You have to learn the rules before you break them.

Only after you've mastered the traditional method can you improve upon it.

412
It's cute when a girl ties a man's tie.

413
Serve meals.

When you entertain, your focus shifts away from your own needs, allowing you to exercise capacities like empathy, imagination, and vicarious experience. The act of serving a meal teaches you to observe others, to anticipate their desires, and to empathize with their experience; it's invaluable and life affirming.

414
One margarita is delicious; two margaritas is a headache.

415

Travel.

As a young woman, instead of saving, I traveled the world. I have never regretted it, and I encourage you to do the same. Wanderlust is a hunger for knowledge—a thirst for understanding of your place in this world. Your journeys will feed it by forcing you to observe, navigate, decipher, and participate. You will learn from being homesick, being seasick, being lonely, and being awakened to the fact that your birth and location are glorious accidents.

416

Cut your losses.

You will make some bad investments, financial and emotional. It's the reality of taking chances—they won't all pay off. Try not to hang on longer than necessary; make space in your life for the next possibility.

417

Know the enormity of what you don't know.

There are more things in heaven and earth, Horatio,
Than are dreamt of in your philosophy.
    —*Hamlet*, Act 1, Scene 5, William Shakespeare

418

Embrace the spirit of competition.

If you focus too closely on the single objective
of "winning," you can become stressed or
discouraged by friendly rivalry. It's human
nature to want to win, but even losing has its
benefits. Taken in the right spirit, competition
provides objective feedback and encourages
perseverance, focus, and camaraderie.

419
There is something bigger than you at work.

Daughter, I can't say your father and I have done much to inject a practice of religion or faith in God into your life. We will be sure you understand both sides of your heritage, and that you learn what God means from two loving families who view worship differently. We also plan to expose you to cultures that fundamentally differ from ours in their relationships with holy spirits. Although I haven't instilled in you a practice of worship, I do want you to know there is something bigger than you at work, heavenly bodies notwithstanding. You are part of a whole: This world is neither indifferent to you nor revolving around you. I wish I could give you more than that. Perhaps when I am older and wiser, I will.

420
Don't fight when you're "hangry."
Hungry + angry = regret.

421

**You will lose some things, and
you will find some things.**

Some will be trivial, and some will be
substantial. Make peace with it.

One Art

The art of losing isn't hard to master;
so many things seem filled with the intent
to be lost that their loss is no disaster.

Lose something every day. Accept the fluster
of lost door keys, the hour badly spent.
The art of losing isn't hard to master.

Then practice losing farther, losing faster:
places, and names, and where it was you meant
to travel. None of these will bring disaster.

I lost my mother's watch. And look! my last, or
next-to-last, of three loved houses went.
The art of losing isn't hard to master.

I lost two cities, lovely ones. And, vaster,
some realms I owned, two rivers, a continent.
I miss them, but it wasn't a disaster.

—Even losing you (the joking voice, a gesture
I love) I shan't have lied. It's evident
the art of losing's not too hard to master
though it may look like (*Write* it!) like disaster.

        —Elizabeth Bishop

422

If you want to be good at something, join the community of people that do it.

Expose yourself to the language of that interest or craft, read the writings, participate in the rituals, and befriend others who do it well. Everyone is an outsider at first, but you must delve into it; you will never excel if you can't commit to the community that exists around your work.

423

Ask questions.

That is how you engage with the people and world around you.

424

Trust your doctor, but don't expect him or her to solve all of your medical problems.

Your grandfather is a doctor, and he compares himself to an auto mechanic: He opens the hood, makes an educated guess as to the problem, offers his best solution, and hopes that it works. Doctors are educated scientists, but they aren't magicians. Search for a doctor you trust, tell him or her the truth, and work together to address your medical issues.

425

You'll need some teenage rebellion music.

A few classics: Violent Femmes, "American Music"; the Who, "Baba O'Riley"; Cheap Trick, "Surrender"; Sex Pistols, "Anarchy in the UK"; Nirvana, "Smells Like Teen Spirit"; Tom Petty, "Free Falling"; DJ Jazzy Jeff and the Fresh Prince, "Parent's Just Don't Understand." I can't wait to hear what you come up with!

426
Keep your eyes open during the scary parts.
If you close your eyes your imagination fills in
the blanks; then it's even more terrifying.

427
Have picnics.
What could be better than a picnic?

428
**Preface a difficult conversation by
acknowledging it.**
A great boss taught me to start by calmly saying,
"This is going to be a difficult conversation,
but it's one we need to have." This statement
addresses the delicacy of a situation and allows
the other person to prepare for the discussion,
while showing respect for the feelings at play.

429

Soak up the sun, but wear sunscreen.

When you get closer to thirty, you will look back on all the magical days you spent on the beach, at the park, or by the pool with wonder at how lovely and carefree and warm and sunny it all was. You'll also look in the mirror and get a little twinge; how easy it would have been to apply one more coat.

430

**If a question is asked and
no one answers, speak up.**

There's no need to be shy. It was asked because someone wants a response.

431

If you find yourself in a position of power, don't let it go to your head.

Certain kinds of people are attracted to power. The more power you have, the more they will want from you; that kind of buildup can cloud your focus. Keep your head on straight; be aware that power and hype and financial success are all transitory. Your character is the only thing you have forever.

432

Before you pick up your towel at the beach, check which way the wind is blowing.

433

Eventually, you become what you read.

It's fun to read escapist magazines and the like, but if they are all you read, it follows that their content will be the dominant information in your head. Put some news and literature in there, too.

434
"Closure" is a myth.
The way you achieve closure is by deciding that it's over. That's all you need to do.

435
We tell stories to share our experience of the world.
Humans use narrative to relate to one another, to reveal our peculiar little universes in the hope of finding commonality. Develop your skills as a storyteller and you will feel understood.

436
Have on hand a bottle of wine, a jar of olives, a tin of cashews, and a bar of dark chocolate, and you can entertain at a moment's notice.

437
It's okay to get angry.
We all have our limits; it's futile to pretend otherwise. Learn to express your anger without hurting anyone so you can release it and heal.

438

Be the second person to leave the party, never the first.

439

Affectation is transparent.

When you rely on mannerisms and artifice to represent yourself, a crevasse opens up between who you are and who you purport to be. As it widens, it becomes off-putting to others and deadening to your spirit.

440

Groom your toes before wearing open-toed shoes.

It's thoughtful to others who have to see your feet.

Understand the difference between values, morals, and ethics.

Values are the rules of right and wrong that live at the core of each person. Values are hard to trace and are instilled at a young age; your values are my responsibility. Morals are your purposeful ideals about bad and good; these are affected by your community as well as by your values. Ethics are a formal system of morals adopted by a group, a code you have agreed upon in order to participate in that community. Each builds upon the former. It is important to evaluate these principles in yourself and others, to understand what you believe and where your beliefs fit in the spectrum of society.

To be virtuous, you must be able to recognize virtue; to see virtue, you must consider what is virtuous.

442
Flip a coin.

If you aren't sure which option to go with, assign heads to one alternative, tails to the other, then flip a coin. If you're disappointed with the result, you'll know what to do.

443
Telling people to "relax" will make them do the opposite.

444
If you have cream that is about to go bad, make butter.

Pour the cream in your mixer and beat it for a few minutes until it separates. Drain the liquid and rinse the buttermilk off the remaining solid—that's butter.

445

**There's a trick to being happy
when you're not.**

Whatever negativity you are experiencing, be
the opposite. If you feel frustrated, act patient;
if you feel reserved, act boisterous; if you
feel detached, act connected. You'll find the
challenge alone is enough to distract you from
your pain, but more important, the change in
your behavior will change your state of mind.

446

**Cultivate a genuine enthusiasm for the
minutia of other people's lives.**

This is how to be a friend.

447

Look at the sky.

We often overlook the soothing blue canopy
that encircles our little world. It's shocking how
many days can go by before you notice it up
there. Take comfort in it.

448

I know you didn't ask to be born.

I asked for it. In fact, I begged for it. And I'm
thankful every day for it, for your life and mine.
You didn't ask to be born; yet you were.
And here you are.

My birthday began with the water—
Birds and the birds of the winged trees flying my name
Above the farms and the white horses
And I rose
In rainy autumn
And walked abroad in a shower of all my days.
—"Poem in October," Dylan Thomas

449

Take it easy.
Sometimes that's all you can do.

450

You will never become who you want to be if you blame others for who you are.

You can spend some time blaming me, and maybe I am responsible; but, regardless, sooner or later you must claim ownership of yourself.

451

Avoid empty threats.

When you make reasonable requests that aren't met, it's tempting to threaten dire consequences in order to get your way. Intimidating people with outcomes you'll never enforce just won't work; they catch on to the hollowness of your warnings pretty quickly. Be consistent if you want to alter people's behavior. Be clear in your demands, set up reasonable benefit-reward structures, and follow through on them. It works with children and adults.

452

**The whole earth is moving
and you're standing still.**

Isn't it amazing?

453

Reinforce the positives.

Emphasize the obvious and expose the
obscure; say out loud what is good and right in
the world. Be a source of joy.

454

**When looking at a sculpture,
observe the space around it.**

There is more to a sculpture than the
material itself. Intangible things like shadow
and light occupy space in this world along
with the solid matter of wood and metal.
Train yourself to peer into this in-between,
to study intention and grasp subtlety.
Negative space exists everywhere;
art is a concrete place to practice
contemplating it.

455
**You don't need to draw attention to your
own beauty or intelligence.**
If you're really all that good-looking or smart,
other people will be pointing it out
for you all the time.

456
Your children are not tiny replicas of you.
It's challenging, but remind yourself to
appreciate them for who they are, not who
you could have been, or the potential you once
had, or the things you never did. Give them
everything you wanted and didn't have, but
don't expect them to appreciate it. At least not
while they are still children.

457
Don't take people for granted.
As you get older you'll realize that it's really hard
just to even make a friend.

458

Avoid overthinking a problem.

It's important to be contemplative, but it can be damaging to spend too much time ruminating. You'll create better theories by actively pursuing information, by participating in the puzzle itself.

459

**When you expect disappointment
it finds you.**

Flood

I woke to a voice within the room, perhaps.
The room itself: "You're wasting this life
expecting disappointment."
I packed my bag in the night
and peered in its leather belly
to count the essentials.
Nothing is essential.
To the east, the flood has begun.
Men call to each other on the water
for the comfort of voices.
Love surprises us.
It ends.

—Eliza Griswold

460
Read poetry.

Not everyone feels up to the task; it might help
to realize you don't have to understand a poem
completely to appreciate it. Reading poetry is
a way of diving into something small to see
how big it is. Try it. See if it makes
you feel something.

461
Nothing worthwhile can be found through a short cut.

462
Forgive yourself your transgressions.

There may be times you look back on your life
and are ashamed of something you see. Forgive
yourself and resolve not to do it again; it's the
only way to learn what you stand for.

463

People aren't either wicked or noble.

As my mom would say: We all have
our moments.

464

Some things are just worth learning.

You will be asked to study things in school that
might seem trivial or obscure. You may ask why
you need to know base pairing in DNA, what
tangible purpose it will serve you to learn it.
Try to satisfy yourself with the wisdom that
sometimes it is valuable simply to know and
understand something.

465

You only get one body.

It's sort of assigned to you when you're
conceived, and you're stuck with it. If you can
learn to love it and take care of it, it's more likely
to take care of you.

466

Draw your line in the sand and maintain your sovereignty.

You have to define your own limits, and you have to defend them.

467

We tend to choose the same type of person over and over.

It's something we do to work through whatever issues we've acquired growing up. You love one person, and it doesn't work out. Then you find someone new who turns out to be just like the first and you wonder how you ended up in the same spot, working through the same problems. This is a pattern destined to be repeated until you finally choose someone to stick with and do the work required to resolve the issue.

468

Talk too much trash and people stop listening.

469
Raise your children as individuals, rather than simply boys or girls.

I don't know much about raising sons—even less than I know about raising daughters. But I do believe we can rid ourselves of old-fashioned gender expectations to create happier families and a more inclusive society.

We've begun to raise daughters more like sons, but few have the courage to raise our sons more like our daughters.

—Gloria Steinem

470
Allow yourself just a little bit of wallowing.

471
You don't need to be privy to every detail to be a friend.

You shouldn't badger people into revealing things they'd rather keep private. Some things need to be processed on their own. Just stand by.

472
Everything works out in the end.

And if it isn't worked out, it isn't the end. This may sound trite, but it makes me feel better.

473
Share your admiration of others without reservation.

Thinking too well of people often allows them to be better than they otherwise would be.

—Nelson Mandela

474
Avoid people who claim to hate children.

Don't be a person who hates children yourself. You are a child now, and you are fabulous— wild and unpredictable, but fabulous. Children represent the potential in all of us. People who hate children are people without hope.

475

If you're feeling blue, a piece of your dad's coffee cake always cheers you up.

You are only one year old, and already you know that your dad is responsible for two things in the kitchen: coffee and coffee cake. I imagine as you grow up, it will always be a special treat when he makes it for you. So I'll tell you the secret: extra streusel! And take the time to cut in the butter.

476

You don't have to let the boys win.

As in any game of skill, you should win gracefully, but boys beat us enough just due to their physicality; don't throw the ones you can win just to feed their egos!

477

Overdress.

If you aren't sure of the dress code, you'll feel better and make a better impression if you're overdressed rather than under.

478
Gossip is toxic.

It's a natural tendency and serves legitimate purposes—connecting you within your own community, relating with others about current events—but too much gossip will leave you feeling empty. Learn to rein it in.

479
You are not alone, and you are not the only one.

Be kinder than necessary, because everyone you meet is fighting a great battle.
—Philo of Alexandria

480
If you wait to be swept off your feet, you may end up standing alone.

We waste time looking for the perfect lover, instead of creating the perfect love.
—Tom Robbins

481

Paint the inside of your favorite costume jewelry with clear nail polish.

No more green fingers.

482

Doubt is a by-product of conviction.

You will waffle from confidence to confusion. Your faith in what you believe will be tested. You will wonder if you are on the right path and consider turning back. Know that, inevitably, a way forward appears. Use these moments of doubt to strengthen your purpose and gather your strength. Savor them.

483

You're never too old to start.

Learning new things may get harder as you get older, but it certainly doesn't become impossible. I tell you this because in college I gave up learning French and guitar, believing I was too old to become proficient. Now I realize I've wasted more than a decade!

484
Know that I am proud of you.
Every halting gesture bursting from your
inexperienced limbs, every novel expression
crossing your upturned face, every syllable
escaping your throat—every moment of every
day I swell with joy at the very idea of you.
And I always will.

485
There are two practical rules of driving.
Look where you're going and see who else might
be going there. Driving is the riskiest thing you'll
do each day; avoiding accidents is really
about paying attention.

486
There will always be one more sunny day.

487
The only guaranteed way to get something done is to do it yourself.

488
Be quiet.
We live in a loud world. We have loud minds.
The only volume you can control is your own.
Turn it down. The old adage often proves true:
The less you say, the more you hear.

489
This is your one life.
Your father and I often stand by your crib in the
dark and marvel that we made you with our
love. That is where you started; it is how you
came to exist. But the rest of the journey is
yours alone to create. You get second chances
but you don't get retakes.

490
Sometimes a size bigger is the right way to go.

I know it's a little devastating to realize you need the next size up, but trust me, you'll look much better in pants that actually fit than you would if you squeezed into the size you wish you were.

491
If you get an unhelpful customer service person on the phone, politely hang up, then call back and speak to someone else.

492
Guacamole is a crowd-pleaser.

In a bowl, combine:

3 diced avocadoes

1 small diced tomato

2 tablespoons chopped onion

1 minced garlic clove

¼ cup minced cilantro

¼ teaspoon salt

2 tablespoons lime juice.

Mash with a fork, leaving a few chunky bits of avocado. Place one avocado pit in the bowl until serving time, and your guacamole will stay green longer.

493

Your father is the standard by which all men will be measured.

He is your greatest protector and your most devoted admirer; fathering you is his wildest challenge and singular joy. Regardless of whether your communication is as strong as you'd like, understand the example he has set through his actions and the impact it has on your perception of men.

There's something like a line of gold thread running through a man's words when he talks to his daughter, and gradually over the years it gets to be long enough for you to pick up in your hands and weave into a cloth that feels like love itself.

—John Gregory Brown

494

Be playful and lighthearted.
Or be dull.

495

There's a science to everything.

496

Sometimes you should be scared.
I'm not talking about entertainment;
I'm talking about life. The scary decisions are
the ones that matter.

497

Every time you rescue someone else, you rescue yourself a little bit.

You will have occasion to save people: to throw a life preserver, to present an opportunity, to alter a destiny for the better. Seize these chances. Reflect your best, most giving characteristics. Rescue yourself from tedious inward focus: These are your opportunities, too.

498

Youth is not wasted on the young.

It is a great tragedy to me that your youth and mine will never collide; what fun we would have had as young women together. I encourage you to be carefree, to be earnest, to swell with anticipation and burst with potential, to celebrate your brief and beautiful youth.

The Cord
I used to lie on the floor for hours after
school with the phone cradled between
my shoulder and my ear, a plate of cold
rice to my left, my school books to my right.
Twirling the cord between my fingers
I spoke to friends who recognized the
language of our realm. Throats and lungs
swollen, we talked into the heart of the night,
toying with the idea of hair dye and suicide,
about the boys who didn't love us,
who we loved too much, the pang
of the nights. Each sentence was
new territory, like a door someone was
rushing into, the glass shattering
with delirium, with knowledge and fear.
My Mother never complained about the phone bill,
what it cost for her daughter to disappear
behind a door, watching the cord
stretching its muscle away from her.
Perhaps she thought it was the only way

she could reach me, sending me away
to speak in the underworld.
As long as I was speaking
she could put my ear to the tenuous earth
and allow me to listen, to decipher.
And these were the elements of my Mother,
the earthed wire, the burning cable,
as if she flowed into the room with
me to somehow say, Stay where I can reach you,
the dim room, the dark earth. Speak of this
and when you feel removed from it
I will pull the cord and take you
back towards me.
                              —Leanne O'Sullivan

499
The measure of your goodness is not the amount of love you receive.

It is the quality of the love you give to others. It takes a long time to learn this lesson, maybe more time than most of us have.

500
Do what you think is right.

I've shared with you this long list of advice: Some lessons I've learned; some tips I've found helpful; some virtues I've tried to embody; some ideals I've failed to live up to; and some things I simply believe to be true. Know that I don't expect or desire you to live your life to the letter of my advice. My intentions are much more tender. I hope this list helps you discover your own way of living well, saves you from unneeded pain, orients you toward purpose, and rewards you with satisfaction. I know this is your life, daughter, and I trust you will live it with conviction and grace.
Do what you think is right.

Acknowledgments

My daughter, Scarlet, you are the window through which I have finally been able to see the beauty everywhere. Thank you for making every day come true.

Joleen, Niko, Clare, Quinn, Madison, Sylvie, Audrey, Tesla, and Flora; your mothers are my safety net, and you are our anchors. Take everything we say with a grain of salt; then chart your own course on that buoyant sea.

To my agent Alison Fargis and editor Patty Rice, thank you for making it rain and helping my dream to grow.

To my chosen sister, Jacinda: You are the reason I can do anything. I wish we had known each other as girls. To my first sister, Jennifer: I did know you as a girl, and despite all evidence to the contrary, I feel privileged. To my newfound sister, Samantha: I am sorry we missed out on girlhood together, but I am proud to see myself in you now. To my sister-in-law Stevee: You are my life preserver, without you I would certainly drown. To my soul sisters Sonya and the women of STAA: You are my rock and my island. To my youngest sister, Rachel: You are destined for greatness, this I know.

To my mother, who chose me: Thank you.

Credits

Andrews McMeel Publishing, LLC
an Andrews McMeel Universal company
1130 Walnut Street, Kansas City, Missouri 64106

www.andrewsmcmeel.com

14 15 16 17 18 WKT 10 9 8 7 6 5 4 3 2 1

ISBN: 978-1-4494-5998-7

Library of Congress Control Number: 2014935268

ATTENTION: SCHOOLS AND BUSINESSES

Andrews McMeel books are available at quantity discounts with bulk purchase for educational, business, or sales promotional use. For information, please e-mail the Andrews McMeel Publishing Special Sales Department: specialsales@amuniversal.com.